JUSTICE IN INDUSTRY

PETER MAYHEW

JUSTICE IN INDUSTRY

SCM PRESS LTD

334 00820 4

First published 1980
by SCM Press Ltd
58 Bloomsbury Street London WC1

Photoset by Input Typesetting Ltd
and printed in Great Britain by
Billing & Sons Ltd
Guildford and Worcester

To John McManners,
Regius Professor of Ecclesiastical History
in the University of Oxford,
who taught me to do research and tried to
teach me to do it well.

CONTENTS

FOREWORD

I am grateful beyond words to Professor David Jenkins and to Dr John Atherton, Directors of the William Temple Foundation, for their devastating criticisms of various early versions of this book. It has taken three years to do the research and writing for the final version.

When I started three years ago, under the William Temple Foundation, I had in mind the idea that justice might be the key to industrial relationships. I had gained this idea from my previous work on the Christendom Group, a twentieth-century group of Christian social thinkers. Also, as a result of my study of them, I had resumed my interest in industrial relations which I had originally worked at under John Hicks at the London School of Economics. I was haunted to some extent by the unpleasant memory of bitter experience of industrial conflict in North Queensland when I was working there in 1961. I had been appalled at the time at my inability in any way to help in the midst of a community with which I was deeply concerned. Now I discovered a passion within myself to discover what really happens on the shop floor.

At the end of a year I produced a tentative first version. The William Temple Foundation were not at all satisfied. In particular, its Directors pointed out to me that I had given no account of good management. I told them that I had not at that time been fortunate enough to find any. I then gave myself a course in good management, with the help of a list supplied by a very eminent body which gave me the names of some sixty firms noted for good industrial relations. I went up north to Edinburgh and Glasgow, to Manchester and (three times) to Liverpool. I went to East Anglia and to Wales, as well as to factories and plants in the Oxford and Greater London areas. Wherever I went, I found myself taken seriously, given generous treatment by management, and (in most places) given every facility for private talks with foremen, stop stewards and hourly-paid workers, as well as opportunities of meeting various groups. All this I greatly appreciated. I kept careful notes of dates, places and persons, and of all that was said to me, in many cases recording on tape what I heard. Where I visited I usually sent copies of my notes to the persons concerned, to ensure the accuracy of what I intended to write about them.

I am particularly grateful to various biblical scholars, teachers of philosophy and of sociology and industrial relations, who have been most helpful to me. Dr Kevin Hawkins, of the Bradford University School of Management, was good enough to check in detail one whole chapter of one of my versions; and Mostyn Davies, a Peterborough Industrial Chaplain, was so kind as to read the whole of one version and to give me verbal criticism which caused me to think furiously. Two former pupils of mine, Jack Lee of the Working Together Association, and Jack Hargreaves of the Department of Industry, were marvellously kind and helpful to me. I am grateful to many others in industry and in the University of Oxford. The research and the writing were for me hard work in the midst of a busy life; yet the whole experience was enlightening and encouraging and almost satisfying.

Peter Mayhew

INTRODUCTION

This book is written primarily to explain what is wrong in industrial relations in Britain, for the benefit of people outside industry who know little about it. It is also written in the hope that some of its content may be read by or passed on to persons who are engaged in industry. It is written with a sense of urgency because the need for improvement in relationships in some parts of industry is very great.

When the Prime Minister of Great Britain chooses to declare that this country has 'appalling industrial relations and the lowest productivity in the Western world',[1] we are surely challenged to consider what is wrong, how much is wrong, and what can be done about it. Let none of us imagine that ill may occur in industry without damage to the whole community. When the American-owned Singer Sewing Machine factory on Clydebank was threatened with closure, the Director in Scotland of the Confederation of British Industry declared that 'it is essential that the Government steps in with all speed'.[2] He went on to say that closure would be 'a disaster, both in industrial and human terms'. The CBI does not appeal for government intervention for trivial causes. The truth is that Britain is a primarily industrial country, and that both its density of population and its relatively high standard of living are based upon industry. Industrial decline means a decrease of population or a decrease in the standard of living (or both).

The Bank of England *Quarterly Bulletin* (not widely read) expresses the present situation with scarcely concealed forcefulness: 'The relative industrial decline of this country is now widely seen as a matter of grave concern. If allowed to continue it would seem only too likely to lead to growing impoverishment and unemployment in years to come.'[3] When, in October 1979, work-force support was needed for the closure of plants and the shedding of 25,000 jobs in the cars division of British Leyland, the Chairman of the company and the majority of the Executive of the Confederation of Ship Building and Engineering Unions jointly appealed to the workers to support the plan. Sir Bernard Scott, Chairman of the Lucas Group, added his plea to the work force. 'Please weigh your responsibilities,' he said. He claimed that more than a million dealers, component suppliers and outside contractors and their dependants would be affected by the ballot[4] of the Leyland workers. The BBC, commenting in its world service on 17 October on this same issue for Leyland car workers, reported that, after taking into account the industries which produced component parts for Leyland, the jobs of 450,000 workers were at stake. Only those without experience of unemployment and its effect upon human beings can regard the possibility of the loss of jobs by so many without acute apprehension. We are not dealing merely with 'industry' but with the lives of a considerable proportion of the nation. Damage to industry is in fact damage to the body politic. A letter to *The Times*, referring to present economic ills, rightly warns us that 'the community that will be destroyed is the whole of the kingdom.'[5]

Until the Industrial Revolution of the eighteenth century, Britain was basically a self-supporting agricultural country, with a relatively small population and with cottage industries where men and women worked with their hands in their homes. As the steam engine began to provide the power for industry in the new mills and factories, the population began to rise from 9,000,000 (as it was in the 1700s)[6] towards the nearly 56,000,000 which it is now.[7] Out of a total of 22,500,000 actually in employment in 1975, more than 7,000,000 were employed in manufacturing industries.[8] This is a very large proportion of the working population. If Britain is no longer 'the workshop of the world', it has at least succeeded in maintaining a share of its industrial eminence. Its exports of manufactured goods in 1976 were valued at over £21,000 million out of the total value of over £25,000 million for all exports.[9] Upon this industry and these exports (with services such as insurance which help to pay for its imports) the British standard of living has been built up. That standard is no longer now as high as that of some of its European neighbours; yet British working men towards the end of this twentieth century now own cars and go (in their thousands) to Spain for their holidays. They have become accustomed to these things.

Sir Nicholas Henderson, formerly British Ambassador to Bonn and Paris, tells us that recent figures of gross domestic production ought to give cause for concern.[10] He writes that in 1954, nine years after the war, Britain produced 22% more in value than France, 9% more than West Germany. By 1977 the French produced 34% more than the British, and the Germans 61% more. The figures, he explains, are based on one price level and constant exchange rates. 'The trends,' he says, 'emerge clearly.' One may quibble at the figures; but British deterioration in relative productivity is notorious. Mr James Prior, Minister for Employment, speaking on 13 October 1979 at a non-political meeting, declared that if Britain 'continues as it has done in the last twenty to thirty years', it 'will become an impoverished nation before long'.[11] Those who discount what politicians say and those who live in a state of false security because of their ignorance of elementary economics may refuse to take Mr Prior seriously. Those, however, who are prepared to face objectively the realities of economics must be obliged regretfully to agree with him.

The Finniston *Report* of January 1980 is concerned principally with engineering. Some of its comments, however, are of broad industrial interest. It declares that 'the importance of manufacturing to Britain's prosperity, and hence to the welfare and living standards of her people cannot be overstressed'. It reminds us that 'manufacturing industries . . . generate 30% of the nation's wealth and employ 32% of the British working population'. It challenges us to compare our relative prosperity until the 1960s with the fact that 'Britain is now poorer than many of the countries she formerly outperformed; and that the roots of that relative decline and the seeds of future recovery lie with the performance of her manufacturing industries'. It goes on remorselessly (and rightly): 'Radical and fundamental improvements in the UK manufacturing performance are required if the rising levels of private and public consumption to which the British people have become accustomed (and expect to continue) are not to fall further behind those in other industrial countries.' It declares that employment and living standards depend critically upon the extent to which British companies can compete in international competition for trade overseas.[12]

The Guardian tells us that the 'British Steel Corporation still has the lowest output per man, and the lowest return on assets of any major steel producer'.[13] It adds: 'British Steel has an appalling productivity record; perhaps the worst in the world. Certainly the worst in Europe. It produces 108 man/tonnes a year, compared with 180 in France and 200 in Germany. This is after five years of capital investment on a scale unmatched in Europe.'[14] The British Steel Corporation can offer closeness to its customers; but its foreign competitors can offer equal or better prices based on higher productivity. For a country dependent upon its exports this is calamitous. The figures are disputed by the steelworkers and their unions. However, the fact that there is overmanning in the industry is incontrovertible.

One of the themes of this book is that the decline of British productivity is due to a considerable extent to failure in industrial relations. In the early chapters I try to show where and how in some industries and in some industrial units relations have been good, and where and how in some others they have been unsatisfactory. I attempt to explain how bad relationships are sometimes the result of human failure to treat fellow humans as they ought to be treated. There is nothing original in this thesis, but I shall try to make the problem real to those to whom it is not at present a real problem by illustrations mostly from my own researches. I shall go on to suggest that there is a structural aspect of the problem. There is a lack of utilization of groups within industry which might become happily involved within their own spheres and increase both a sense of community and productivity itself. I shall explain and argue this very carefully. After dealing with examples of both good and bad industrial relations, I shall suggest that there is a way forward which is both philosophically and religiously authentic: that of the conscious adoption of the principle of justice as a commonly agreed basis for consultation and negotiation. I claim that along these lines both sides in industry can achieve a 'high trust' relationship within an industrial community that will minister both to the needs of men and to the need of industry itself.

I am a Christian who believes that Christians should try to understand what is going on in the industry which is vital to the well-being of the people of this country. Christians sometimes have influence among their fellow men. Christian men in management and Christian shop stewards, among others, certainly have influence within industry. Christian preachers preach the gospel all the better if they have some knowledge of the working lives of the people to whom they preach. Representatives of the church who visit the homes of the people will be none the less effective if they show a little interest in (and perhaps a little knowledge) of the conditions under which the men and women in those homes work. Christians sometimes fail to talk, or fail to talk sense, about things which matter to men, because they have not attempted to acquire knowledge or understanding of the ways in which men spend the greater part of their lives: at their work. The moral is obvious, the need for understanding great. Inspiration is wanted to bring new life to this land and people, to this present day declining industrialism. This book is intended to suggest a way of inspiration.

1 Wonderland

This study of industrial relations is concerned primarily with industry in Britain. Let us, however, now, at its beginning, go like Alice into Wonderland. Let us look at an extreme case of a breakdown of industrial relations which occurred in May and June 1979 in a remote iron mining area in Western Australia. At the end of this study, we shall look again at an Australian scene, but at a very different one. We shall see another kind of mining area, one for lead and copper, in the far north-west of Queensland, an area where I lived and worked in the early 1960s, and to which I returned for a few days in June 1979. In between the beginning and the (happy) ending, I shall confine myself to Great Britain.

On the table in front of me lie many documents concerning a dispute in the Australian winter of 1979 at Hamersley Iron Pty Ltd, in the remote Pilbara district of Western Australia, more than 1000 miles from the capital, Perth. I was in Australia during this dispute, and I did my best to use my eyes and ears in respect of what was going on in industrial relations at Hamersley Iron ('incorporated in Victoria', but with its Western Australian head office in Perth). The dispute was over the re-negotiation of the agreement between management and unions which was due at that time. The Hamersley Iron 1977 *Iron Ore Production and Processing Agreement* is contained in a small book of over 170 closely-printed pages. It had been signed by Messrs T. R. Lynch and T. Barrow on behalf of the company, by eighteen representatives of the Australian Workers' Union, and by seven other representatives of Western Australian branches of national unions. It was to bind for two years, and envisaged a subsequent negotiation after 30 June 1979.[1] In its 'Introduction' the company promised sympathetic disposition 'towards considering a negotiated reduction in the normal standard hours of work', provided that the man-hours lost because of strikes was (over each of the twelve-month periods subsequent to the 1977 Agreement) kept down to 'less than half of one per cent of the available man-hours that should have been worked'.[2]

On 1 May 1979 the company and the unions agreed to begin negotiations at Paraburdoo on 28 May for a new Agreement. On 10 May the representatives of the eight unions concerned sent to the company office at Perth their eighteen pages of 'logs of claims' for the new Agreement; they declared their willingness to meet representatives of the company for the purpose of negotiating the claims as from 28 May 1979. These 'logs of claims' were served on the company in Perth on 14 May. However, in relation to their first four claims, the unions stated that they were 'not prepared to negotiate'. They required positive answers from the company prior to 21 May 1979. These claims included a 'paid meal break for all workers', a change in the redundancy clause, and 'a sick and accident scheme totally financed by Hamersley'.[3] Another claim was for 'a 40% overall wage increase'. This, they stated, was 'negotiable'; but they sought 'an indication from the company as to their position, prior to 21 May 1979'.

On 23 May, Mr T. R. Lynch, Manager, Industrial Relations, sent from Perth to the Hamersley managers in the Pilbara district a brief account of the unions' and the company's tactics. The company had in fact, he said, replied to the unions by the required date, 21 May. Mr Lynch complained that the unions were making certain items 'the subject of demand rather than negotiation'. He stated that the company had refused to yield in advance of nego-tiation to these 'demands'. It had submitted counter-claims to the unions. 'All claims,' he said, 'must be negotiable and the final package deal will reflect the results between us.' The company sought a three-year agreement, and offered 'paid communication meetings to each union at each site, of up to two hours each alternate month', subject to continuity of operations. The unions then circulated to all their members a statement that the company had 'refused' their five most important claims. The statement was signed by three representatives, from Dampier, Tom Price and Paraburdoo respectively, representing the negotiating team which had met in Paraburdoo on 22 May. There had not at that date been a mass meeting of the employees. As a result of various subsequent meetings, there was a strike and shut-down of oper-ations as from 8.30 a.m. on 24 May.

Mr Lynch, in a circular to 'all employees who are on strike', protested to the workers: 'Through your unions, you have made your claims upon the company. Some of those claims were stated to be "not negotiable", which is certainly an unusual way to try to negotiate. Now you are trying to deny the company a right to make its claims and we have even stated that all our claims are negotiable. Collective bargaining is a two-way event. It cannot be a one sided "stand and deliver" demand. It does require that both parties give and take in achieving the eventual compromises which usually occur when negotiations have been successfully concluded. Put bluntly, you have gone on strike without even a commencement of the negotiations. Therefore no changes will occur to the existing Agreement whilst your strike continues and the start of negotiations is aborted. The Agreement will, in any event, remain in force until 30 June. We had hoped to replace it with a new Agreement by concluding negotiations before 30 June. You are now wasting that time and opportunity.' Mr Lynch's assumption was that a new Agreement, similar to the 1977 Agreement, could have been reached by give-and-take negotiations between 28 May and 30 June. Mr Lynch concluded: 'We will not negotiate whilst you are on strike.'[4]

An unsigned document circulated 'to all concerned' proceeded to charge the unions with striking 'before negotiations even began'. It also charged the company with delaying its counter-claims which, it says, could have been made earlier than 21 May (so that 'the troops could have enjoyed the holidays with their kids!'). The company, the document said, was losing contracts, and the unions were losing jobs. The document aroused much curiosity. The general opinion was that it was not inspired by the company. It expressed to some extent what many were feeling: an apprehension concerning the course of events and future prospects.

On 22 June, the company made conditional offers which were partial concessions to the unions' demands. On 25 June, however, the unions decided to remain on strike indefinitely; the Tom Price Combined Unions Committee Women's Auxiliary (TPCUCWA) reported to its members that on that day 'an overwhelming majority on the three sites voted to "hang in there" until we win'. On 26 June the company withdrew its conditional offer by means of a 'Notice to all employees', signed by the General Manager, Operations. The company stated to its employees on that date that 'it will not now persist with its attempts to achieve the negotiation of a new Industrial Agreement. From our point of view, and the position in which we are left by the repeated refusal of the Unions to negotiate, we have decided that negotiations are now neither practicable nor possible.' It added that 'the company will not accede to the ransom demanded by the Unions'. After 30 June 1979, said the company, it would apply to the Western Australian Industrial Commission for the making of an Industrial Award and the specification of terms and conditions of employment to be determined in arbitration by the Industrial Commission.[5]

In our wanderings in Wonderland we have moved fully into the orbit of the Australian States' industrial laws. I left the country on 27 June. A week earlier a 'Co-ordinating Committee' based on Karratha and Dampier had begun to make arrangements for the supply of free vegetables and meat 'for people in difficulty' and for supplies 'at cost price' for families who were 'without income'. The Co-ordinating Committee at Dampier arranged for single men 'with no incomes or savings' to be given $5.00 each week (on Thursdays). A family with no income or savings would be supplied with $10.00 a week in addition to groceries (on Tuesdays).[6] The Australian dollar is worth approximately half an English pound. The Tom Price Combined Unions Committee Women's Auxiliary (TPCUCWA) stated that: 'We are here to see hardship is overcome. . . We are a voluntary service and wish to help. If you have any problems, such as shortage of food; come and have a chat with us. . . There are ladies in your area willing to listen to your problems and give assistance where possible.' There was, of course, no dispute pay; and it seems that there were 'shortage of food problems'. The ladies would be 'there to assist you every day except Tuesday and Friday mornings'.[7]

The repercussions of the dispute were Commonwealth-wide, owing to the arrest by State police of two allegedly Communist union officials who addressed a meeting of strikers without due authorization. The people of Australia were concerned lest Commonwealth-wide union action in support of the union officials might affect them adversely. Otherwise, the Hamersley Iron strike seemed of little concern in Australia (except in union circles) and of none whatsoever anywhere else.

In fact, the Hamersley Iron strike is worth looking hard at as a type. However brash the conduct of both sides in the Pilbara district of Western Australia, underneath that brashness there lie attitudes all too common in more sophisticated industrial contexts.

The threats, the actions carried out to prove that the threats were serious, the obvious counter-actions, the hard and bitter words, all these are to be seen and heard in Britain. The lack of interest of ordinary people in what was happening is also to be found in a British public opinion which usually blames the unions and then tries to forget.

The Hamersley Iron dispute (and others like it) demands Christian concern and reflection. Lack of Christian interest in Australia concerning Hamersley was dismaying. I worshipped on Sunday 24 June in a church in Brisbane; there were no prayers (perhaps there were no thoughts) for the people of the Pilbara district of Western Australia. The previous week the Synod of the diocese met at the Church of England Grammar School in Brisbane. Away in Western Australia, hard-earned savings were being eaten up; bitterness and fear were growing; relationships between people of the same stock but on different sides in the dispute were being damaged; a mining community was being torn apart. The Synod of the diocese of Brisbane had more important things to talk and pray about than the affairs of a remote area of a far-away Australian state. Yet remoteness ought not to excuse lack of concern. The Christian believes that in such clashes of men with men the progress of the kingdom of God is retarded and the God who was wounded in Jesus is wounded anew. Theology is not invariably of the transcendent.

This book is intended to make an especial appeal to 'the Christian', whether he be worshipper or sympathizer. It suggests that he ought to be concerned about all sorts of human relationships, including those of industry. Reinhold Niebuhr wrote that 'a part of the Church, fearing involvement in the ambiguities of politics, has abandoned modern men in the perplexities of the modern community and has seen brotherhood destroyed in a technical society without a qualm'[8]. The Christian ought not to be concerned only with what is normally called evangelism, with bringing men to the knowledge of God and to the acceptance of Jesus Christ as king and saviour within the fellowship of his church. Evangelism is in fact about the gospel; but the gospel is about the kingdom of God, in which God's laws are to be kept and his will done. The Christian ought indeed to be concerned with the creation of an order in which God's rule is recognized, in which men are encouraged to treat their fellow human beings as God wills them to be treated. God, the God of the Christians, is concerned with men's attitudes to one another as well as with their attitudes to him.

Rowan Williams rightly tells us that we ought to accept 'this complicated and muddled body of experiences as a possible theatre for God's creative work'.[9] Professor David Jenkins says that the Christian should consider very seriously 'the incredible possibility and gloriously exciting mystery that God is actually involved in and committed to the actualities of human existence as men and women experience them in any and every age'.[10] He adds that 'our central theological hypothesis is that a necessary way to discover contemporary and effective Christian sense is to get to grips with that which significant numbers of our fellows find themselves to be in the grip of'.[11] Elsewhere he writes that there is an 'agony and urgency' about the need which calls for 'developing hopeful activity and continuing criticism'.[12] There is indeed amongst newspaper readers, amongst industrialists and managers and trade unionists, a feeling that we are in the grip of something which impedes both industrial progress and the growth of community in this country. This book will suggest that we ought not to be altogether without reasoned hope of improvement, of freeing ourselves (or of being freed) from such a grip. To join in such a hope, to participate in such a search for what is true and right, is surely a Christian responsibility and the responsibility, too, of all men seeking to create community in society.

2 Misconceptions

Before beginning to consider aspects of British industrial relations which inevitably damage British industrial productivity, we need to rid ourselves of some common misconceptions. Good, intelligent, well-educated persons, ignorant of industry and misled by the news media, often make generalizations concerning industry which have little foundation. Among the most common of these is that the British worker is strike-prone, that he is work-shy, that the unions are invariably anti-employer (if not anti-work). Let us deal with each of these allegations in turn.

The phrase 'the British disease' is used sometimes to describe what is alleged to be the habit in British industry of resorting to industrial action too quickly and irresponsibly. *The Australian* ('published in Canberra and circulated by air throughout the Commonwealth') defines the British disease as

> a virus which affects industrial relations so that the instinctive reaction to any dispute, major or minor, is angry aggression. As a result, we have strikes, walkouts, stopworks, go-slows and all manner of disruptive action taken without any attempt at looking to the wider effects of such actions, at thinking about whether a business or the whole economy will be shattered as a result, whether others will lose jobs or whether production costs will be so affected that nobody can afford to buy whatever it is we're making – an article or a national image.[1]

Let us look hard at some relevant figures. The Department of Employment, in its official *Employment News* of January 1978, declared that 'in an average year 98% of the factories in Britain have no strikes'.[2] A Department of Employment press release of November 1978 states that 'even during the whole of the period of high strike activity in 1971–73, 95% of plants were found to be strike free'.[3] These are very high percentages, and they concern the 1970s. The Department's figures for 1977 include only 2703 recorded stoppages of work begun during that year.[4] These figures are surprisingly small for a country with a working population of 26,300,000.[5] It needs to be borne in mind that stoppages of work for less than a day do not qualify for the official record. Nor do stoppages involving less than ten persons, unless they result in the loss of a hundred or more working days.[6] The Department's *Gazette* for November 1978 concludes that 'strike activity is extremely concentrated'.[7] It goes on: 'A small group of industries and geographical subdivisions suffer relatively high levels of strike activity, and strikes in the manufacturing industry are concentrated in a relatively small number of large establishments. Conversely there are large sections of British industry with very few strikes, which is very different from the popular image of widespread and frequent strike activity.'

In 1977 the number of working days lost and the number of workers involved in strikes in the motor vehicle industry were more than double those of any other industry in the country.[8] The engineering workers' industrial action in 1979 and the thirteen-week steelworkers' strike in 1980 draw attention to the fact that the bulk of British strike activity takes place in large-scale industry and in large units of production. One of the themes of this book is that this concentration of bad industrial relations in such industries ought not to be inevitable. It is, however, true that such industries are in particular need of good management from that at the top to that on the line. They are also in an especially good position to train such management.

The epidemic of strikes in early 1979 (the 'winter of discontent') was primarily one of low-paid public service workers revolting against a threatened 5% wage increase at a time when inflation was nearly 10%. They received much publicity; but they were scarcely typical of British industry. The *Financial Times* noted that, while more working days were lost during the first quarter of 1979, there were in fact fewer stoppages and fewer workers involved than in the same period of 1978.[9] No one would have guessed this from the more popular news media.

The *DE Gazette* for February 1980 declared that official International Labour Office figures showed that 'over all industries and services UK strike losses in 1974–78 averaged less than half a day per employee per annum'. That is strikingly small. The same

figures show (according to the Department) that the United
States, Canada, Italy and Australia all 'lost relatively more working days than the UK'.[10] The Department went on to say that
'despite a marked rise in UK strike losses in 1979, this overall
assessment may not be greatly modified when averages for the
years 1975–79 become available'. One is bound to add that by the
end of the year 1979 just over 30 million working days had been
lost. This was the highest number of days lost in a year since 1926,
the year of the General Strike. It compares with an annual average
of 10.6 million days over the previous ten years.[11] According to
the *DE Gazette*, in the 1979 'winter of discontent', public service
strikes cost 3 million working days; later the engineers' strike cost
16 million. 11,249,000 working days were lost in the month of
September 1979, the highest monthly total since 1926.[12]

Again, it is interesting to note on this subject the comments of
Mr Van der Vat of *The Times*. He told me that he was asked by
a deputy editor to examine for his paper the reason 'why the
British worker apparently strikes so readily and so often'.[13] Mr
Van der Vat's article, written after considerable research with the
Industrial Relations Department of Warwick University, the Con-
federation of British Industry, the Trades Union Congress, the
Advisory Conciliation and Arbitration Service and the Institute of
Personnel Management, showed that the underlying assumption
was untrue. 'I set out to talk to as many relevant sources as I
could and came to something approaching the opposite conclusion.'[14] Mr Van der Vat in his article quotes the Chairman of
ACAS as referring to the 'generally inaccurate' conception of the
nature of strikes; and he himself mentions the enormous amount
of space devoted rightly or wrongly by British newspapers, radio
and television to strikes. He affirms that British strikes 'are almost
always local, small, and of short duration and, despite all the
publicity, they usually come as a shock to both sides'. He concludes, as a result of his painstaking investigation, that 'our reputation for striking is undeserved – because it is at variance with
the facts'. A close study of the figures over the years, he declares,
does 'permit one clear conclusion: that the British, when it comes
to strikes, have nothing to boast about, but also are nothing like
as bad as they (and many foreigners) like to think'. If the strikes
in Britain in early 1979 dispelled any such relative optimism as
Mr Van der Vat was attempting to assert, nevertheless the news
media must bear some responsibility for the unfairly pessimistic
popular conception of strike-ridden British industry. Those, for

example, who live in Oxford gain from the local press a picture of British Leyland as seldom free from industrial action of some sort. In fact, there are in Oxford many BL workers who have had jobs at Cowley for twenty years and have never yet been on strike. I live in Oxford and know some of them.

It is easy for those who have professional jobs to condemn persons less secure than themselves for strike-proneness. Some outside industry are quite ignorant of the legitimate role of industrial action when it serves (as it frequently does) to bring to an end a situation in which there has been prolonged tension and mistrust, leading to poor productivity. Indeed, Dr Kevin Hawkins, an associate member of the British Institute of Management, and Lecturer in Industrial Relations at the University of Bradford Management Centre, declares that in his opinion the unions have sometimes exerted 'too little pressure from the shop floor'.[15] He believes that strikes are sometimes necessary to improve conditions. Pay and working conditions are perhaps not good enough; productivity (as well as happiness) would be increased if they were improved; and a strike may be the best means to attain all these ends quickly. It may indeed be the best way to a more secure and trusting relationship. It is, of course, difficult for people outside industry to realize that a settled strike does sometimes clear the air.

Nothing written here is intended to minimize the significance and seriousness of strike action. It is only that there are actions of workers which may signify as much in their context as a strike, and matter more. Behind all action there is probably some unsatisfactory condition. Restrictive practices are often concerned with work groups rather than with their unions.[16] Very frequently, very effectively, they seriously hinder the efficient use of labour.[17] They consist chiefly of bans on overtime, working to rule, and go-slows. *Work Place Industrial Relations 1973*[18] reports considerable 'forms of pressure of this sort during the year', basing what it says upon the evidence of both management and shop stewards. None of this can, at least in the short run, benefit industrial relations. The existence of these forms of pressure helps us to see that strikes may be only the obtruding tip of an iceberg; the news media concentrate upon exposing that tip; but under the surface there lies a considerable mass of discontent. Such a state may well not be typical of British industry as a whole; but it is real, especially in many of the multi-plant industries. It is a fact that when there is genuine discontent, not all men can afford to strike, to risk

losing their jobs. Two members of a group of Bristol sociologists
at a strike-free chemical plant in western England (which they call
'Chem Co') describe the attitude of a discontented but non-militant work force: 'Most men plod along, making the best of a bad
lot. They do not expect to be happy at work but their pay could
be worse. They see no point in getting into an argument and
jeopardising what little they have. . . 'Seeing no sign of society
changing, they follow what for them is the simplest and most
sensible course.'[19] They work on without heart or energy, resorting at times to all sorts of action and inaction, but taking care not
to lose their jobs. There is slackness and apathy; there is wastefulness and sometimes vandalism; there is an utter lack of 'caring'
about anything at work, an almost total non-involvement; there
is a determination to 'get by', until eventually they can get out.

With reference to the charge of work-shyness sometimes laid
against British workers, the writer of the leading article of the
Spectator for 29 July 1978, under the heading of 'The retreat from
work', declared that 'there really does seem to be a profound
disinclination on the part of the British working class to work'.[20]
This judgment was repeated, without comment, by the BBC that
evening in its extracts 'From the Weeklies'. A courteously worded
letter[21] to the editor of the *Spectator*, asking the leader writer to
substantiate in some measure his accusation, was ignored. The
charge of a profound disinclination to work could and would be
refuted by a host of employers and managers in this country. The
Delta Metal Company, for example, in its *Report* for 1977, declares that amongst its employees there was 'widespread co-operation and much hard work'.[22] Delta employs more than thirty
thousand persons. The Hon. G. H. Wilson, Joint Managing Director, confirms that 'the majority of our workers work very hard'.
One wonders what the writer of the *Spectator* article would have
made of the pictures of the long procession of lorries driving from
Carlisle to Birmingham on 24 January 1979 during the truck
drivers' strike. On the front of the radiator of the leading vehicle
were the words: 'Work is not a dirty word. We want some of it.'
The British worker in fact will work as well as his neighbour
(better than some of his neighbours), given work-provoking conditions. Graham Turner, of *The Daily Telegraph*, in a series of
articles during July 1979,[23] again and again quotes foreign tributes
to the good hard work of British employees in Germany.

Lastly we must face up to the benevolent but ignorant vagueness
with which many good and intelligent persons, often authorities

in their own spheres of mental activity, permit themselves to be misled by the news media and fail to attempt to ascertain the facts concerning industry. They castigate 'the unions' as trouble-makers, solely responsible for industrial disputes. A distinguished academic, with an international reputation for his scholarship, declares unequivocally that 'the unions' are to blame for the industrial ills of this country. He has no clear idea of what he means by 'the unions'. He does not know or think whether he means the national leaders, the full-time area officials, the locally elected shop stewards, or the unionized work force as a whole. He does not know, and has not sought to learn, how trade unions are organized or how industrial relationships work. He has, however, his personal vision of 'the unions' as unreasonable, anarchically-minded, probably communist-inspired. A member of a BBC forum condemns stop stewards as 'men who will not work'. He is loudly cheered by his studio audience. It is apparent that neither he nor the audience has any knowledge of what a stop steward is and does. He speaks, they cheer, in ignorance. I have studied the work of sociologists and researchers better qualified than myself. I have tried to do my own research as thoroughly as circumstances have allowed, realizing that much of it has been of the sort described as 'the conversations which journalists snatch', which inevitably compares unfavourably with the 'labours which scientists undergo'.[24] However, the amateur may sometimes have the good fortune to see, hear and record significant things, including considered and unconsidered words of men and women of sincerity on both sides of industry. In these respects this amateur has been singularly fortunate. I have discovered that some aspects of industrial relations are far better than the news media would have us believe, and that some are even worse.

The Right Hon. Barbara Castle, after all her experience as a Cabinet Minister in Labour Governments, reviewing in 1977 *Living with Capitalism*, by two of the Bristol sociologists, wrote: 'How remote we politicians, economists, and theorists are from life as it really is on the factory floor.' For her, she said, the book spelled out the sense of loneliness and stress amongst the workers, the 'sour frustration, fear of unemployment, boredom, resignation, and, above all, non-involvement'.[25] The book itself (educative for others as well as for Mrs Castle) quoted a worker on his job: 'You know it gets really hot up there. Once you've got all your equipment on it's fucking killing to go inside there. You say to them: "Look, it's fucking hot in there. I could pass out or

something." All they ever say is: "It's your job. It's up to you." '[26]
Many good people just have no idea what it is like on some shop
floors, in some plants. Also some good people may not know how
people talk under such conditions. But this is for real.

3 People

I have tried to remove or reduce some common misconceptions over the alleged strike-proneness and work-shyness of the British employee and the alleged non-cooperation of the trade unions. Generally speaking, these allegations are simply not justified. Yet the hard facts remain that British productivity is low, and that this is in part due to unsatisfactory industrial relations. 'Industrial relations,' says Dr John Atherton of the William Temple Foundation, 'are the major contributing factor.' As industrial relations are about people in industry, we must look hard at various sorts of people; and we must look especially hard at the majority group in industry, that of the hourly-paid industrial worker. We must try to understand his characteristics and his human needs; we must try to estimate his likely reactions to various situations and approaches; we must realize that there will always be a certain unpredictability about these reactions because of his very humanness. We must also look hard at those who manage him, who are in positions of authority over him; and we must see if those who are in such authority can be helped in some ways to understand better those under them, to exercise that authority in a manner which works towards the common good, including both relations of fellowship and high productivity. Of course, the importance of human factors in industry has been recognized and talked and written about before this, especially by the 'human relations school' of industrial relations writers. For those, however, who are unacquainted with industry, there is a tendency, encouraged by the news media, to generalize in too facile a manner, about the workers, the employers, the unions. Different men in different groups react in different ways. Great sensitivity is needed in the understanding of men in industry; great delicacy is required in the handling of them. Although many books and articles have been written about industrial relations, I am going to suggest that some have been written unrealistically. I am also going to suggest that some American writers of high idealism may sometimes write what sounds good but does not work.

However, first and foremost, I must say quite plainly that there is a basic need in industry for both corporate structures and individual functions to be so arranged that the worker feels involved. He needs to have his interest aroused, to sense that his interests are being respected, that his capacity is in some measure being fulfilled. 'That's my ship,' said the young Sunderland worker. He had helped to make it. An older worker on Clydebank echoed him as a ship was launched. 'My heart goes with it,' he said. A friend of mine standing by overheard him say it very quietly.

I watched a year ago a young man high on a ladder cleaning windows on a science building in north Oxford. He worked with speed and vigour. Eventually, I went over to him, and asked him why he was working so hard. He was, very rightly, not prepared to spare me much time. His answer was simple: 'Because I'm a window cleaner.' That explained itself. Here he was in a job where he seemed to fit, and he was doing it to the best of his capacity. He was involved. We shall see later in this study that even in large-scale industry, even on the assembly line, it is possible for workers to feel involved. But it needs care in the selection of men for the job, it needs trouble in explaining what it is all about, and it needs a good deal of encouragement along the way.

The Joint Managing Director of an important engineering group, the Delta Metal Company, declares: 'The Group's success depends largely upon people. The people are the Group.' There are 32,000 employees in that particular group. 'It's bloody people that industrial relations are all about,' said an Edinburgh senior shop steward in the course of an informal discussion at which I had the privilege of being present. A young manager in the same plant on the same day, struggling to express himself, said that a worker just had to be thought about as a person. The remark has a conventional sound; it was in fact, from him, passionately sincere, the fruit of both bitter and heart-warming experiences. Workers are not always thought about as persons.

One of the most common causes of bad industrial relations is the misunderstanding of persons by persons. It may happen because parties do not meet very often and therefore cannot know one another very well. It may be because of different social and educational backgrounds which may be thought to make common understanding difficult. They do not make it impossible. People with the same background may still misunderstand one another. The Edinburgh senior shop steward (who is branch chairman of his union) opened the informal discussion with a fellow senior shop steward and two representatives of management by speaking of 'still existing class barriers'. He did so in the midst of this small group in which all who spoke used the same language in the same way and came from the same sort of homes and schools. It gave one cause to think hard.

A group of persons with the same social tradition may develop misunderstanding which affects relationships and impedes that spirit of co-operation which is vital in industrial production. Here is a case in which a social triviality became the cause of anger, hostility and wastage of time. It remained unforgotten, the ridiculous symbol of division between 'them' and 'us'. Three representatives of a Liverpool firm, a manager and two senior shop stewards, were staying in a hotel together in 1976 for the purpose of making an inspection on behalf of their company. After dinner, the management representative stood a round of drinks with money provided him for this purpose. One of the shop stewards then asked for some of this money, so that he might stand the party a round. When this was refused on the ground that it was the firm's money and not the manager's, the party broke up; the shop steward went angrily to his bed. When, later in the year, the shop steward told the story in the presence of the same manager, the latter still appeared incapable of understanding the cause of the shop steward's indignation. It is this kind of insensitivity, sometimes a seemingly sheer inability to comprehend, which constitutes an odd sort of 'non-class barrier'. Men may graduate into management from the shop floor, and then develop characteristics which seem to separate them from those with whom they once worked. (Some, of course, do nothing of the kind.) In the hotel drinks case, real hostility was generated; the memory of the incident lingered. The person outside industry who imagines that strife is all to do with trade unions knows little of how, amongst humans in industry, trivialities may be blown up with no help at all from trade unions or anyone else.

Sometimes there are (probably unconscious) attempts at 'blowing up' by the news media, especially for many by the television news. Humourless faces of stern and unbending employers talk with grimness or pomposity from the screen; they would do better

not to speak at all. Angry, frustrated senior shop stewards, men
of violence seemingly (but by no means in fact) reply with ferocity.
'Types' of management and of unionists become established on
the screen and in viewers' minds. When one meets these men (on
both sides) they are quite different; they show signs of openness
and reasonableness of a kind not in the least suggested by their
screen images. The media speak of management, of the employers, the unions, as if these were of predictable and unchanging
ideas. In fact the hard-faced business man and the hard-headed
trade unionist can speak and act in surprising ways, sometimes
because they themselves are taken by surprise. When human
beings made aware of one another's humanity come into close
contact they may change their minds about one another. In the
case of the Edinburgh discussion, there was a basic liking and
respect for one another on both sides. This was despite the allegation of still existing class barriers. A relationship of quality was
difficult but practicable because both sides saw much and knew
much of one another. The shop stewards were not Communists
or International Socialists; nor did they resent the higher incomes
of the management men. They were all on Christian name terms
with one another. They belonged to a firm where there was recent
history of improvement in relationships.

Yet here, as elsewhere, apparently inevitably, management had
adopted a different life-style from that of the hourly-paid workers.
With its higher incomes, its inter-managemental social life, its
traditions which new members quickly acquired, management
men were just different. As a result, a problem was constituted,
a barrier had been, willy-nilly, erected. Such barriers can only be
overcome if they are very frankly faced. Unless there is great
sensitivity towards those who feel the barrier, it may become a
serious impediment in the way of good relationships. The other
Scottish senior shop steward present said that 'there's got to be a
change of attitudes'. There can be changes of attitude amongst
wise men. As one feels towards another, one begins to feel with
him.

In contrast to this Scottish firm with high ideals and much
human wisdom amongst some of its managers is Chem Co, which
my friends, Theo Nichols and Huw Beynon, describe in *Living
with Capitalism*.

We have already had a terrifying look at Chem Co in chapter
2. Here, under the façade of a 'New Working Arrangement',
relationships were almost non-existent. In theory, management

took industrial relations seriously. 'Human beings,' said a manager, 'are our most important piece of machinery – like machines, if you don't keep them running, men will go rusty.' Indeed, managers were expected 'to acquaint themselves with a new technical literature – on the psycho-sociology of work'.[1] In Chem Co, NWA meant the 'New Working Arrangement'. A Chem Co press statement said that 'we see NWA as doing something together, with people, not to people'.[2] It declared: 'We want to involve employees in the creation of new arrangements for doing work.' That sounded good. Yet, according to the researchers, managers and workers all contrived to be involved to an almost minimal extent. In fact those who had been involved in the not so distant past had become in the researchers' time a subject of legend. There had been 'Phil Lancaster'. He had a Ph.D. He was a plant manager who worked with his men. They said of him that 'Phil had the human touch'. They said: 'He was a *real* manager, a man's manager.' The men added that 'he might as well have lived on the site'. Called in on a Sunday afternoon, 'he jumped right in there, best suit and all, up to his knees in shit'.[3] So the legend went. 'Now,' say the researchers, 'Phil has gone.' So to a large extent has his style of management, they add.

It had become company policy at Chem Co to push managers away from the smells and noises of production into offices at some distance from the works. 'The Company leaves the day-to-day running of the plant in the hands of its production foremen, who . . . are responsible to the site shift manager. The foremen, unlike the plant managers, spend all their time at the plant.' Experienced managers, the researchers tell us, know that the office is their territory. 'Desks, chairs, secretaries, coffee (and biscuits), telephone calls: these are all part of their world – not the world of the shop floor.' The plant managers were provided with differently coloured bicycles (with their names painted on them), so that they could cycle over to see the places where the men worked. In their offices there were 'diagrams and equations of many colours'. These are men at the hub of chemicals as a science-based industry. 'They monitor labour as a cost . . . and they see men less. . . They don't set foot on the plants all that often; they spend most of their time on policy issues and any necessary local union negotiations.'[4] An almost inevitable growing away of middle management from the hourly-paid workers had taken place. The researchers found cases of terrible alienation. They described one young plant manager 'with a brilliant degree in chemistry', aged

28 in 1970. He spoke with contempt of his workers. He described
some of them as 'u/s, defective'. His opinions were forcibly expressed and generally well known. He called his men 'idiots' if
they failed to 'understand'. 'He was seen to epitomise the new
bright, ambitious "whizz kid".'[5]

Perhaps something needs to be said in defence of the authors,
both of whom I know and respect. Their book is a competent
study, based on prolonged and thorough concentration by a team
of researchers upon a plant with a small work-force. It gives a
vivid picture of an unsatisfactory industrial relationship. Nichols
and Beynon are university sociologists, now working in different
universities. At the time of the research for the Chem Co project
both were teaching in the University of Bristol; and the plant was
situated conveniently for them. They spent three days each week
there over a period of three years; their two research assistants
were there daily throughout the period. They were permitted by
management to speak freely to all persons on the premises. Theo
Nichols told me that they carefully noted (and in many cases tape-
recorded) conversations with management and with 118 hourly-
paid workers. Over this three-year period they inevitably established relationships. They sometimes went out drinking with the
workers, sometimes visited their homes. They were allowed by
Chem Co to talk to men during their working hours; and, the
researchers working in pairs, they sometimes talked to a man for
two or three hours. Eric Batstone, of the School of Industrial and
Business Studies at the University of Warwick, says that 'this is
an important book in terms of describing work experience'. 'It
breathes,' he says, 'a sense of reality.'[6] Richard Hyman, of the
same university, writes that 'as a work of sociological analysis,
Living with Capitalism is certainly of major significance'.[7] James
Mortimer, Chairman of the Advisory Conciliation and Arbitration
Service (ACAS), writing critically, admits that the evidence revealed by the two sociologists cannot be disregarded.[8]

The physical separation of plant management from plant workers at Chem Co was the symbol of a separation in mind and spirit.
In theory for Chem Co there was a 'dialogue and day-to-day
relationship'.[9] In fact there was little meeting of bodies and none
at all of minds. Frequent meetings of bodies give at least an
opportunity for a meeting of minds. It is difficult for good relationships between management and employees to grow, if the
workers do not catch much sight of the men over them who make
the decisions. A distinguished company director, Mr G. A. Peers,

stressed the point to me that crises are best settled between people who are used to meeting one another outside times of crisis. Indeed, he said, no crisis may arise at all (for example over annual pay negotiations) if representatives of the two sides are in frequent contact.

At the Edinburgh meeting of management and senior shop stewards referred to earlier in this chapter, both sides were used to contact. Yet the tension was there, the sense among the shop stewards that something might be happening which they were not prepared for. There was the defence mechanism of men in an inferior position, not entirely trustful of those above them, a little suspicious. Despite the obvious and genuine friendliness of the two management men, there might be someone higher up in the hierarchy 'getting at them' in some way. It was an interesting and significant atmosphere; and there were fascinating reactions as that atmosphere gradually changed during the course of the meeting. Coffee was served, and was commented upon with some surprise by the stewards. Before the end of that ninety-minute meeting one of the shop stewards said with great emphasis: 'We want the company to produce.' He was identifying himself fully with management's goal of productivity. The other one said (with a smile): 'It's still a good company to work for.' Both meant what they said, but it had taken ninety minutes of managemental presence at its most open and charming, with coffee and cakes, to bring them to this point. All concerned left the meeting happy, relaxed, tired. I was exhausted as a result of the prolonged sense of tension early in the meeting. It was the end of an exercise conducted amongst men whose social backgrounds were similar, and yet amongst whom class distinction was still felt by the workers' side. On both sides there was honesty and sincerity. There was on the managemental side a genuine and determined effort to bridge the gap; there was in the end a warm and generous response from the shop stewards; the time and the effort required revealed the extent of the gap. There was a uni-status canteen in that brewery; management queued up with workers for food and non-alcoholic drink; yet division remained.

'Class' in itself, differences in speech and social customs, create no insuperable barriers. Where there are differences of speech, they may be an initial but they need not be a permanent obstacle. In 1912, R. H. Tawney wrote that 'there is no provision that our employers shall understand the language of the people they govern.[10] In 1980, Sir Keith Joseph, the Industry Minister, declared without originality in the House of Commons that 'there is an absence of mutual understanding between management and workforce in this country that lies behind strikes'.[11] It may not have been a very profound observation, but it was certainly significant and true. It is also true that understanding can be achieved. Language barriers can be overcome (as international statesmen sometimes learn).

When just men from the two sides of industry are in frequent contact, and have discovered their common humanity and their common concern and respect for one another's humanity, all sorts of surprising developments become possible. A young railway worker recalls how he and his mates agreed that 'you couldn't do enough for a good boss'. The General Secretary-elect of a trade union testified to me with enthusiasm for the validity of this remark. A tough and militant convener, a senior shop steward of twelve years' standing, spoke without sentimentality of a manager who 'went down well with the lads'. He said simply that 'we knew he'd look after us'. All these words were spoken spontaneously during 1978.

Time does not alter human problems (although training can make some of them less insuperable). In Stafford in March 1980 a young service engineer remarked of the factory manager for whom he was working: 'Mr S. knows how to treat people.' He added, quite without bitterness: 'Some bosses just don't want to know you.' Later in the same month, a talented young research student in need of a helping hand towards new work, remarked with gentle tolerance of his supervisor: 'He wouldn't concern himself.' I was angry. What chance for involvement, what hope for understanding, for working together, for community?

Out of the 1979 Christmas cracker came the aphorism: 'Never claim as a right what you can ask as a favour.' I met Neil Wilson again after many years that same year. He is a haulage proprietor on the 'Sunshine Coast' of south Queensland, and he has ideas about how people should handle people. Physically hardened, his face lined in early middle age by the dust and wind on the cracked Queensland roads, he is sorry that he is not paying his men 'what they're worth'. One day he and his fellow proprietor mean to pay them more. In the meantime, management and men work together. He says: 'If they've got something to say, they say it – bang.' He adds: 'If I go crook on them, they just laugh.' The business expands; it keeps its drivers, gains new ones. Neil Wilson says: 'We don't tell them. We always ask them.' Sometimes he says to

a man: 'Do you reckon you can do the job?' He may add: 'I've
done it myself.' All his contacts, he says, are verbal. He says (and
means) that he keeps everything honest and above board. 'It pays
off,' he says. He works hard by day and night, looks older than
his years. He says of his men: 'We trust them completely.' He
himself is simple, shrewd, experienced, tough. I felt better for
meeting Neil Wilson again. He has learned management in a hard
school; one would want men to learn the same lessons in easier
schools. He gives us a clue or two about good management. What
is possible on a small scale is not necessarily impossible on a big
scale. Within large industries and complexes there are relatively
small units. The management which deals with the small groups
in the big complexes needs to be good, well briefed, really well
trained. The representative of management in a small group bears
great responsibility.

On indeed quite a different scale is Pehr Gyllenhammar, of
Volvo. Here is an employer who claims in no uncertain terms that
for him people matter. There was considerable discussion (and
variety of conclusion) on the shop floor of the Assembly Plant at
British Leyland, Cowley, the day after an article appeared in the
Sunday Mirror concerning Volvo's Kalmar factory.[12] In this article
the head of Volvo stated to John Knight (of the *Sunday Mirror*)
that his factory was designed 'to make everyone happy'. 'Thickly
carpeted rest rooms, sauna baths, the odour of freshly-ground
coffee', and above all good working conditions had helped to
bring absenteeism down to 4% (according to the article). British
Leyland workers in Oxford asked if it was real.

Pehr Gyllenhammar moved from insurance to become President
of Volvo in 1971. He claims that he is 'trying to place people
first'. He writes that they are not to be treated as educated au-
tomata but 'as human beings with enormous potential'. He declares that if people are made subservient to machines and
systems, they will react in very human ways. Gyllenhammar claims
to care for the importance in work of 'personal development, the
chance for individuals to learn more, to enhance their personal
lives'. He writes that the humane treatment of human beings at
Kalmar has 'helped create for employees a sense of
membership'.[13] He wants the worker to be relaxed at work, to
feel in a sense his own master, to find happiness in his daily work.
One is bound to add that the high rate of absenteeism, which
(*pace* the *Sunday Mirror*) is well-known to be typical of Volvo

plants, causes the student of industry to question the extent of the
success of Mr Gyllenhammar in realizing his ideals for his workers.

As we shall see more clearly in the next chapter, a step by step
approach to human problems, as these problems show signs of
arising, may be considerably more effective than an approach
from theory. Let us consider the manifesto of a British group,
part of an American-based international company, Tannoy, of
Coatbridge, near Glasgow. The Tannoy Group Limited, in a 1976
statement of its philosophy of management, declares that one of
the two prime goals of the company is 'to create working conditions which are both pleasant and fulfilling for employees at all
levels in the company'. The statement goes on: 'The principle of
individual fulfilment expresses our recognition of the uniqueness
of all the people in our employment and the wish to allow them
as far as possible to use and develop their individuality through
their work.' Tannoy's four principles are summed up in their
statement as 'security, fairness, individual fulfilment, and
involvement'. These are the British version of the 'Bolivar
principles' of the parent American company, Harmer International: 'security, equity, democracy and individual fulfillment'.[14] The
British development of these American ideas was codified in the
statement drawn up by Norman Croker and by Jim Hughes, General Manager at Tannoy, and by a management team assisted by
Mary Weir, of the Work Research Unit of the Department of
Employment. From the start of work at Coatbridge in 1976, the
group and the General Municipal Workers Union (GMWU) co-
operated. Both the union and the workers believed (and believe)
in the sincerity of the General Manager, Jim Hughes. His personal
principle is that 'you have to be committed to it.' He is committed.
His concern for the job security of workers at Coatbridge is
'passionate', as a worker assured me.

Researchers are common at Tannoy. The researcher may read,
see, hear, for all he is worth; maybe with benevolent scepticism.
On the other hand, the union branch secretary at Tannoy, a silent
canny Scot, sees and hears more, and writes to me: 'My own
feeling is that with this type of approach, we the work force feel
we are being treated like human beings. When you spend most of
your time working in jobs which do not require skill . . . to be
treated as a human being is good for your self-esteem.' The philosophy of management is being conscientiously, indeed devotedly,
put into practice; yet there is grating where it does not quite fit
the need. Indeed, industrial relations depend upon the wisdom

and sensitivity of thoughtful men rather than upon philosophies of management. High managemental principles are not enough; they may not meet workers' innate needs. What these needs are and how they can be met can only be discovered in each situation by the intimate co-operation of management and workers, as they feel their way towards that fellowship in community in which there is involvement and personal fulfilment. A worker frustrated in a firm whose management is pledged to workers' participation made a desperate plea: 'You need people who understand people. That's all we ask. Be prepared to understand.'

The late A. J. Jenkinson, Senior Dean and Fellow of Brasenose College, virtually the founder of the School of Philosophy, Politics and Economics in the University of Oxford, gives a fascinating account of a Ministry in the First World War seeking to increase the production of munitions, initially without either philosophy or experience of management.

> The Ministry, which at first looked only to production, endeavoured to become a model employer. The welfare of the munition worker rather than his mere efficiency became the end. The principle of fair wages was extended and a national minimum prescribed for women employed on munitions work. The canteen became an integral part of the national factory, and private establishments were encouraged to follow the example of the Ministry. The amenities of the factory were studied, and special officers were appointed to look after the comfort as well as the health of the work people.[15]

The output of munitions increased. The Ministry had felt its way towards success.

It is not the spectacular or the sensational which makes for satisfaction, for fellowship, for peace in industry. Rather it is primarily the treatment of workers as people who matter. (We shall see later on that there is even more than this to it.) At the Greene King Brewery at Bury St Edmunds, where almost every worker is a union man (and yet there is no closed chop), not one worker referred to the annual 'treats', the trip to the sea-side, or the Christmas hamper. There was, however, mention again and again of the 'availability' of management and of its quickness to respond to need. 'They always listen to what you say,' a fitter operator told me. 'If it is really worrying they get on to it right away.' He added that it was not like his last place (where he was a foreman). There, he told me, they would say: 'Don't bother me now. I've got to pop out. I'll see you when I get back.' 'Here,' he said, 'there's always help.' A foreman explained to me that everybody gets a hearing; a shop steward said that all stewards had access to all management (so long as they went through the right channels). He added that members of management were welcomed at the monthly shop stewards' meeting if they wished to bring up some point. Sometimes it was a help to the stewards when they wished to make a complaint; sometimes it was a help to management to have the opportunity of making an explanation. Again and again, I heard the word 'family' being used to express the atmosphere of this firm (with its three breweries, its three depots and its expanding trade).

It might be possible for other employers at this end of the twentieth century to think along these lines, to consider possibilities, the adoption and adaptation of what works well in relationships elsewhere, without committing themselves either to printed statements of intent or to the risk of endangering profits. R. H. Tawney wrote in 1912 that 'the indictment brought by workers against modern industry is . . . that under present arrangements men are used not as ends but as means'. He went on to plead for 'security and opportunity . . . a fair chance of leading an independent, fairly prosperous life'.[16] The French sociologist, Georges Friedmann, of the Conservatoire Nationale des Arts et des Métiers, wrote that the challenge to modern industry is the humanization of it.[17] It is impossible, he said, to create around the daily routine of work a general atmosphere of contentment . . . which can be called 'professional satisfaction'.[18] Tawney, in his Economic History lectures at the London School of Economics in the early 1930s, had spoken of the need to give to industry a sense of being a profession. If there is to be professional satisfaction in industry and professional standards, there must be a recognition that the professional man is a trained man, a man educated in his profession. Industrialists, industrial managers, shop stewards, all need to be trained for their jobs.

Industrial relations itself is a science requiring study, an art to be acquired. If men are to learn to co-operate with men, men's minds must be carefully studied. Friedmann wrote of 'the link between the technical, the psychological and the social', and of the dependence of industry 'upon personal psychological elements'.[19] This really means that some knowledge of what is commonly called psychology must be acquired. Much can be learnt from experience; but often this way of learning is lengthy, costly, painful. On the other hand, Professor Douglas McGregor, formerly of the Massachusetts Institute of Technology, wrote wisely that 'few managers are competent to practice psychotherapy'.[20] It is not, in fact, psychotherapy which is required in industrial relations, but a simple basic knowledge of the workings of the human mind, of human behaviour problems. The Director of the Industrial Society (which works for good industrial relations and organizes many courses for management, supervisors, shop stewards) writes that on these courses tuition is normally by 'people who have practical experience of industry'. I have vastly enjoyed taking part in one of these courses, which often include role-plays demonstrating the wrong and the right ways of conducting meetings, of bargaining and negotiating. These role-plays may be well acted and are usually helpful to all who are present, and the (mostly) young men who come to such courses are often ready and keen for more. They are frequently hungry for knowledge of how best to do their jobs and willing to learn all they can about the working of the human mind (even more than about industrial law or the Advisory Conciliation and Arbitration Service). Dr Alan Fox, of the Oxford University Department of Social and Administrative Studies, tells me from his experience of the keenness of young management trainees to know what they can give and do to help to generate trust-relationships in industry. I too have observed this. Nigel Nicholson, of Sheffield University, writing in *The Industrial Relations Journal*, similarly describes newly-elected shop stewards' readiness to learn.[21] Yet he is obliged to note the complete absence in courses available to them of any attempt to provide behavioural skills. On the Top Management course at Cambridge in September 1979 an experienced and intelligent young manager from Kenya, who had disagreed with me on several points, was emphatic in agreeing with me on the need for the study of psychology on management courses. He declared that this was never provided. Another young man, this time from Zaire, agreed; but he warned wisely against the danger of acquiring a little knowledge of a big subject. Management courses demand (and deserve) good teachers; and psychology requires good teaching. Management courses are expensive; the good teachers and teaching ought to be provided.

Management often looks on management courses as 'perks', according to an industrialist. He was thinking primarily of the Administrative Staff College and the Harvard Business School. He looked with interest and cynicism at the programme of the

Top Management course on my desk. 'What hope?' he said. It was a reasonable question. In a three-week course, lectures were daily from 10 to 12 noon, and from 2.30 to 4.30 p.m. A total of two hours was to be given to 'Personnel Management and Industrial Relations'. So much for that. On the other hand, David Waller, Second Brewer at Greene King's, feels that good management is not likely to be the fruit of management schools. 'Management skills', he says, 'are intuitive – a personality thing.' Indeed, he thinks, a manager must depend on personality. He finds it difficult to imagine the case of a manager lacking strong personality and yet still capable of learning through good training.

It is easy to deride management (and other) training courses. The non-professional man reacts against professionalism. Young men returning from courses are frequently told that now they can 'get down to reality' (presumably after a period of unreality on the course). An Australian puts it rather crudely: 'So now you've been on a fancy human relations course. Get out there and kick arses.'[22] The seeker after good industrial relations sometimes feels a sense of near despair when and where he perceives admirable engineers and metallurgists and other highly trained experts having difficulty in understanding and coping with human beings. D. H. Carroll, a warranty assessor at BL, Cowley, claims that 'management development' means persuading every man in management at every level to concentrate on improving his own performance and that of those under him. He is saying that managers are made, not born. It is not so very long ago that Professor Allan Flanders testified to the Donovan Commission that 'Few managers have been prepared by their education or experience for the social aspects of their function . . . Labour relations have therefore been conducted in almost complete ignorance of the Social Sciences and frequently on the basis of the most primitive dogmas about the determinants of behaviour'.[23] Leaders on both sides of industry deserve and are in need of the very best kind of training; and both sides ought to take the behavioural sciences seriously. British industry, men in management and trade unionists, it must be repeated, need more training than they get in the understanding of human behaviour. When asked whether his managers received training in management, an Operations Manager spoke with sincerity of the respect which he and his fellow managers had for the dignity of their workers. He told me, with pride, that many of his managers were graduates and that all were assessed annually. He had somehow missed the point. I was inquiring about their training in the art of management. If there is need for the study of engineering, need for the learning of skills in the working of machines, how much more needs to be studied and learned about the human being who is to be managed. The painstaking acquisition of knowledge about him ought not either to be neglected or derided. Teachers are rightly taught in Colleges of Education about the subjects they are to teach, about how they are to teach them, and about the persons whom they are to teach. They are taught psychology. Men on both sides of industry need to be taught how best to handle one another with that respect which demands knowledge of the humanity with which one is dealing.

This chapter has been an attempt to stress the importance of maintaining and developing respect for the humanity of all engaged in industry. In the last part of the chapter it has been urged that the human mind needs to be carefully studied if human beings' capacities are to be adequately used and their needs adequately met in industry. However, it must be obvious that proper human care for the individual is not all that is required if industrial relations are to improve. Industry is not a glorified Boy Scout Troop. We have to consider very seriously the role of the trade union in industrial relationships. This I shall attempt to do in later chapters.

4 Management

Let us now look at some examples of how people behave towards people in industry, beginning in this chapter with management, and passing on in the next to shop stewards as the most significant representatives of trade unionism.

There is a banal statement often made by representatives both of management and of the unions to the effect that the function of management is to manage. It is sincere amongst those workers who realize management's working hours and the heavy responsibilities that go with those long hours. They do not care to share such burdens. Sir Michael Edwardes, Chairman and Chief Executive of British Leyland, declares: 'I work very hard because I think that if I don't work very hard and my top team don't work hard – we may not succeed.' He adds: 'I am sick and tired of pushing and driving top managers in this country to work long hours and over weekends.' To management and employee representatives in Birmingham on 1 February 1978 he declared: 'If management looks for a compromise every time, and doesn't set a positive lead, we will go down the slope. . . If one listens to the debates and then decides on a line, this isn't autocratic management – this is the job of managing, and I believe the whole work force is itching to see more decisiveness and more success.' He added: 'Those decisions management is there to take they must take.' The senior shop stewards present did not challenge his words. They accepted this traditional view of management. John Power, an Oxford BL senior shop steward and convener, had already written to *The Sunday Times* to say that: 'Michael Edwardes deserves all the support he can get. His policies are the last hope.'[1] These were strong words for a man with a reputation for adverse criticism of management. An ACAS report on Scottish and Newcastle Breweries Limited, where there had been a dispute in the Tyneside sector of their operations, states: 'We did not encounter any denial of the company's responsibility to plan, organize and manage the operations of the company in order to achieve and maintain maximum efficiency.'[2]

Bill Morton, branch secretary of the TGWU and convener at Glacier Metals, Alperton, has personal experience of both the managemental and the union 'sides' of his company. He says: 'Management must never abrogate responsibility. Management should manage.' Again and again we hear from trade unionists the traditional view that management must take the decisions. Yet this parrot cry is sometimes voiced by men who at another time will be pleading for (or demanding) some say in decision-making, on the grounds that only so will they and others become really involved in the work. There is in fact confusion in some trade union thinking. We shall see in chapter 8 (on participation) how necessary it sometimes is for workers to have some share in the responsibility of managemental decision. Management cannot operate alone if it wants a work force which is in any real sense involved (and productive).

What, in fact, responsible labour is really requiring of management when it asks it to manage is that it should give a strong, responsible, informed and informing, hard-working lead to its workforce. Dawson Piper, formerly a father of the chapel in the Society of Lithographic Artists Designers and Engravers (SLADE), in the presence of Brian Thornburn, a National Councillor and on the executive of the union, assumed his fellow unionist's agreement when he said to me: 'I appreciate good management.' Graham Turner, who has written a good deal on industrial topics and who used to be the Economics Correspondent of the BBC, believes very strongly that men respond to strong management, to managers who 'have guts'. He quotes a factory manager who was unattractive in appearance and personality, and yet, through his capacity to make managers under him do their jobs, raised the spirit and the productivity of his factory. He overheard a notoriously militant senior shop steward say of him: 'There's a man I've got to take notice of.' Michael Houston became mine manager at Ardlethan in New South Wales in 1976. Union leaders said then that one manager was no different from another. Relationships were so bad that Houston could not risk putting his car into his own workshop for repairs. When he left in 1979, men said that they would never get another manager like him. They told me that his good management had brought about a complete change in the attitude of the work force.

Graham Turner quotes a TGWU shop steward, David Mitchell, who said: 'I prefer a manager that speaks his mind because then you know exactly where you are.'[3] In the same article he mentions an assembly worker who says that he prefers not to work for a manager who is 'soft'. In another article he refers to a national union official who said to him: 'It's up to management. If they don't manage, the workers will do as they please. If they do manage, the workers will respond.'[4] In fact we know that it is not enough for a manager to be clear and definite; he must also be wise. A former chairman of the American Inland Steel Company writes that the outstanding characteristic of the good executive is his capacity first of all to make up his mind and then to translate thought into action. However, he adds most significantly that his decisions must reflect wisdom.[5] Wisdom is not innate but can be acquired by the perceptive. If management is to play a leading and responsible role in industry, it need not possess technical expertise; but it needs to know what it is doing; and it must have the capacity to assess and to make reasoned criticism.

At a small engineering works in the Midlands, a new young Managing Director makes it his business to go quietly on to the shop floor and sometimes to question the workers. He tells them that he does this because he 'wants to know'. He explained to me: 'It isn't matiness. I want to learn from them.' An intelligent apprentice commented: 'Mr A used to say "Hullo, how are you?" Mr B shows real interest.'

Trade unionists who are inclined to assent to the maximum managemental authority and responsibility in theory are likely also to assume that in practice management will also take counsel, knowing that amongst its own workers both wisdom and experience are often to be found. We shall see that even if management must, after consultation, take the great policy decisions, labour may reasonably be allowed to take some of those shop-floor decisions for which the knowledge and experience of shop stewards equips them. After all, as Douglas McGregor wrote, 'every manager at every level is dependent upon those below him in the organization'.[6] To recognize this is to begin both to spread and to breed responsibility.

There are, of course, managers who do not know when to stop interfering. Huw Beynon and Theo Nichols, writing of Chem Co, tell of the manager who, the men said, 'would always be down here (in the control room) altering the bloody running of the plants'.[7] They go on to recount how on one occasion 'Mike turned round to him this once and said, "You bloody alter that again and I'll wrap it round your bloody neck" '. Part of the art of managing is to be able to help without interfering, to be able to interfere when necessary without hurting. This art has normally to be acquired. When it is not acquired, by persons who imagine that there is no need to study it, the result is tragic.

On the other hand, there are managers who really do not qualify to manage. Graham Turner, with considerable experience of variety of industry in Britain and overseas, gives examples of managers who have in fact abrogated their responsibilities. He quotes a painter from Crewe on contract to Lufthansa speaking of management as he had known it in England: 'Manage! In England they don't. They're too fond of slipping off for lunch and coming back three hours later.'[8] He mentions a shop steward who declared of managers: 'If you don't see them, like some places, they're strangers to you, a wall comes up between you.'[9] Graham Turner spoke to me of a senior union man who had suddenly realized that the personnel manager to whom he was talking had never even been into the factory. He had been in the job for nine months, but he had been 'too busy' to go into the factory. The union man could scarcely believe it. Turner himself feels strongly that men are usually very happy to see a manager with his sleeves rolled up.

He mentions in one of his articles a German executive, Karl Ernst Kalkbrenner of Porsche's: 'In English factories, I feel it's a cold atmosphere. . . Time, attention, affection – if you don't give those to your people in the factory, it will go down.' Turner asserts that this was said (and practised too, there in Stuttgart) without sentimentality. Turner himself strongly believes that the British worker depends upon personal relationships, that he needs someone at work to whom he can relate. He tends, he says, all too often to be working in a totally deprived emotional atmosphere. 'It's a question,' said Herr Kalkbrenner to Graham Turner, 'of management, of organization, of incentive.'[10] John Coffey, a carpenter now working in Gothenburg, told Turner: 'If they only put their hand on your shoulder and made you feel like somebody, you'd be only too happy to work for them.'[11]

Let us look now at some examples of good management, as it succeeds in the challenging task of being both efficient and humane. In a north-country cigarette factory we find all levels of management conscious of the respect due to the human beings who, with tobacco, paper and machinery, are concerned in the process of the production of cigarettes. The factory manager's large office is within a few yards of one of the two shop floors. He himself is on and off the shop floor throughout the day; eight or nine times a day sometimes, he told me. He spends as much time as he can in the factory because, he said, 'contact is essential'. As he does not want to seem to be usurping the supervisor's job, he usually has him (or her) with him when he is on the shop floor. He believes that his presence is always noted and that men and women working there have always a fair idea of what he is doing there. He is as conscious as anyone of the 'fantastic pressure of office work', of the 'endless meetings', of his responsibility for the financial success of his factory. He is determined in a competitive (and a threatened) industry to fulfil that responsibility to the full, for his company's sake and for his own. He also recognizes his personal responsibility for all relationships within his factory. He says that 80% of his job consists of human relationship problems, and that he refuses to have an 'us-they' situation. He believes in the payment of respect due to authority; and he tries to help to build up the authority of those in the factory who are in management and supervision. He encourages those who work for him to understand and recognize the role of each person in authority at each level, to know the 'determining manager' appointed for each function where decision is required. He does not encourage 'leap-frogging', in the sense of going to higher authority to avoid the designated authority lower down the hierarchy. He does not believe in managemental weakness or sentimentality at any level. He himself has been factory manager for twelve years; his assistant manager has had more than forty years with the company. He believes in the need to maintain continuity of management, and claims that there has been very little movement within his team, because of the job satisfaction found within it. He knows his people in this factory of 1200 workers; he is conscious of the pressures of automation, of the agonizing effects of job insecurity. He is determined that reduction of the number of employed shall only be made 'at an acceptable rate'; he knows that 'insecurity makes for an unhappy work force'. He also recognizes that seemingly trivial complaints need to be taken seriously, because they may well be symptoms of deeper and more significant (but unmentioned) grievances. In his factory there have been no strikes since 1961.

The employee relations manager (for this and another near-by cigarette factory) is responsible, among other duties, for passing on information to the factory managers. These pass it on to management beneath them, and so it comes down to the supervisors. Those 'forgotten men of industry', says the employee relations manager, are treated as important means of communication between management and the shop floor. They are encouraged to have the kind of relations with the shop stewards which will promote the whole process of communication. 'My job,' he says, 'is relationships.' It is the firm's policy to recruit management from the supervisors as far as possible. The employee relations manager is responsible for the organization of training. There are internal courses for probationer supervisors, and there are also courses in London on a national basis for line management personnel. These courses, he explains, include the study of human relationships and the behavioural sciences.

A recently promoted shift manager, keen but a little tense, tells me with enthusiasm that he hopes to be in the factory till he retires. He adds: 'I never thought of going anywhere else.' He came to the factory as a young maintenance fitter. For seventeen years he has worked with his shift-making supervisor. He says that those who work with him know his capabilities. In fact, 'we all know one another so well'. He does not believe in being in his office for more than 20% of his time. He does not believe in swearing at those who work for him. ('Swearing should be kept for great occasions.') He himself is 'totally involved'; and he believes it is possible for everyone else to be totally involved. He claims that a lot of suggestions come from the shop floor. He says that anyone can stop the shift manager and speak to him. He adds (with simplicity and conviction) that he cannot fail, because of the people he has working with him. He regrets the lack of training in behaviour patterns on his management course, but he believes that he has in fact learnt a great deal about human nature from his long experience with the company. There was a frankness and honesty and quiet enthusiasm about him.

The shift-making supervisor working under him realizes both the importance and the delicacy of his relationships with the shop stewards. He recognizes fully the right of those who work for him to go to their shop steward with complaints and problems rather than to him. He says, on the other hand, that he would love them to come to him – in fact 99% do come to him. He tries to listen to everyone, and is determined to treat people as human beings.

He always attempts to ask them courteously rather than to order them. He believes that a 'man's heart is in the job if he is asked in the right way'. He believes that his workers do not resent his supervision. 'If someone does wrong, you speak firmly and quietly . . . you get people working better if you treat them more tolerantly.' He does not regret the days when workers were expected to call the supervisor 'sir'. He says that he notices with interest that people laugh as they go to work. He knows that workers recommend the factory to other members of their families. 'Whole families work here,' he tells me.

The branch secretary of the Tobacco Workers' Union speaks of 'nineteen strike-free years in the factory'. He says that this is a combined success of management and unions. He seems to mean this. I talked to him by himself, when he was under no pressure. The factory's senior supervisor, a woman, agrees. She refers with enthusiasm to the fact that management goes up from the shop floor. She talks about the monotony of the work, but she believes that this is redeemed by a twelve-minute break in every working hour. She says of her workers that 'if you explain, they'll bend over backwards for you'. She remembers with distaste how, in her early days, she was not allowed to eat or smoke in the factory. Now, she says, there are tea rooms and rest rooms, and the money is good. She says that she is fond of people, loves her girls, and would not dream of going anywhere else. She provides reliefs and pass-outs for her workers when she can. She believes them to be happy and she is happy herself.

This is a quiet factory which does not proclaim a philosophy to the world. Its factory manager describes those in authority as 'QBE' (qualified by experience). It seems to illustrate the remark of Lord Allen, a veteran trade unionist (of the Union of Shop Distributive and Allied Workers), who claims that 'more management should be recruited from the shop floor. . . , people with understanding of trade unionism and experience of everyday working life'.[12] Those who manage (and those who work) in this factory do not talk much or write at all concerning their ideals; they get on with the job. If, however, they are pressed to talk, they do so with realism and frankness. Here is competent and conscientious management.

In our continuing study of management which proclaims to the world no philosophy or principles but which is in fact first-rate, we move further north. At the keg plant of a brewery in Scotland, conditions of work in the 1960s were unsatisfactory and there were frequent stoppages. 'Things happened in that place,' its former manager told me. The plant had earned a bad name and not many people wanted to work there. The work itself consisted chiefly of filling kegs with beer and lager. The kegs then had to be taken from the production line and loaded on trailers for distribution to the regions. The plant was capable of filling around 90,000 11-gallon kegs and 7000 36-gallon kegs a week. The kegs had to be unloaded when they returned empty. For the most part, unskilled labour was employed. In the central yard of the area, where the loading and unloading took place, the men were closely controlled by two foremen to each shift, in the ratio of six men to one foreman. Workers tended not to approach foremen about their problems. Past experience had led them to believe that they were unlikely to receive a helpful reply to their queries. Indeed they had some basis for fearing that they would even suffer victimization if they developed problems. The company became influenced by the 'evangelical lectures' of John Garnett (of the Industrial Society). It decided to introduce 'briefing groups', in order to put workers more fully into the picture concerning the work of the brewery. The new plant manager co-operated fully, but he realized that the situation did not merely require better communications. He himself was prepared to look very hard at conditions of work within the brewery. When he had gained the confidence of a personnel manager of outstanding energy and enthusiasm, 'a great personality' (he told me), he was ready to begin.

He did not start off with a policy. 'There was no management meeting to say that we'd do the following; things just happened.' He started by dropping in at the bothy (the room where the men ate), just to see how they were living. He saw that the chairs were old office chairs (and broken ones at that). Unostentatiously, he replaced them with new, non-office, chairs and he put in decent tables too. He learned to talk to the men in the bothy. He 'just tried to know the men better'. 'The thing,' he said, 'just moved on.' New colour schemes were introduced and the place began to look better. There was a determination that conditions should be upgraded. Showers were put in. There was a decision that somehow or other plugs for the wash-bowls should be there, that toilet-paper should be where it was needed (despite petty pilfering). The men's safety-clothing was improved and men who were cold at work were given track-suits. Management was determined that these things should be done because it was right to do them (and not because of union pressure). This was not paternalism; the manager did not claim intuitively to know best what was good for the men. It was just that he came to see what was needed. He saw the men, listened to them. When he became aware of need, he tried to see that the need was met. There were consultative meetings; at some of them he was abused, and from those in particular he learned how the men were feeling, what they were wanting. It was scarcely a philosophical approach, but it was an increasingly sensitive one.

In all the manager did, he was encouraged and aided not only by the personnel manager but also by a senior shop steward, a truck driver, an unmarried man in his thirties, a dedicated person. Manager and shop steward saw together what they should do next, and together they did it. When the two of them knew what ought to be done, it was already as good as done. The senior shop steward had things said about him, and sometimes he seemed to be making himself unpopular with those who had elected him. When this happened, he would resign. He would promptly be re-elected. That is how things went. It was very real to him as he recalled it all; it became real to me as I listened.

As the situation developed, the manager found that he could speak more and more easily to the men. When he went past the open door of the bothy and saw men sitting in there during working hours, he would say that he gathered that for the time being they had no work to do and had come in to keep warm. If they were taking it easy in the plant, he let them know that he assumed that they were, very reasonably, having a couple of minutes off from their heavy work. This was not intended as sarcasm; there was nothing mean about all this. It was a manner of speaking men understood. 'Why should I have to chase you round the premises?' the manager asked. He told the men that he genuinely believed that they were better than they thought themselves. Those were his words. They knew what he meant. 'You want trust,' he said, and he himself was prepared to give it. He made himself unpopular with some of the supervisors, who felt strongly that he should not allow himself to be abused by the men. In the plant as a whole there was a ratio of one supervisor to between seven and ten men. Broadly speaking, it was true that the supervisors were not helpful to the men. All too often, 'bugger off' was their response to a legitimate question or appeal for help. On one occasion the manager himself witnessed a supervisor's reaction to a man who had been injured and had been sent to hospital. He came back to report to his supervisor that he had been told to stay away from work for a time. The supervisor told him to 'fuck off'. The supervisor knew the manager's policy, realized that he had been overheard, went white in the face. The manager decided that supervisors should have another chance to build up trust, that they should have a specific time each week during which they should be in their various control rooms for the purpose of dealing with men's problems.

Later on, with the agreement of the foremen in the yard, he decided that (on a trial basis) foremen should stay in their office, while the hourly-paid workers got on with the job. They could go to the foreman when there was a problem with which they could not deal satisfactorily themselves. He discovered that the men could in fact be trusted to check their own loads. The era of 'autonomous work groups' was arriving. It was discovered that they could work honestly and well without the supervision of foremen. Many of the foremen were near the time for retirement and were happy to accept it under the company's schemes. Several of them were redeployed to other areas within local production departments of the same company without any loss of income and were not replaced. The whole thing was found to work, said the manager. There was efficiency of production, and there were no more wildcat strikes. Disputes were easily handled within the company's disputes procedures and men no longer felt it necessary to have stoppages of work.

We have arrived, with this young and competent manager and his autonomous work groups, at a development of vast importance. He was not only treating his workers decently, humanely; he was giving them responsibility, as if they were rational beings capable of responsibility. He was giving these trade unionists, these hourly-paid workers, a share in a sense in management itself, and they were responding. We shall see more fully, in the chapters on shop stewardship and on participation, that it is not only necessary for men to be treated with the respect due to human beings. It is also necessary for their varying human capacities for responsibility to be given to the maximum. Those who have the capacity to manage themselves (or others) must somehow be involved in management. By the use of this capacity they become more fully involved in the welfare of the firm which employs them. We shall see later just how important a principle for industrial relations this is. The young manager in the big plant took his risks and was rewarded.

The directors of the brewery said to him and to the personnel manager: 'All right, you pair of firebrands. We'll support you.' They intimated to the manager: 'On your head be it.' In fact, they gave generous support to the experiment, and allowed their two colleagues a reasonably free hand. The senior shop steward had his difficulties, sometimes with management, sometimes with the men. On one occasion management suspended him, but the incident ended with an apology and a handshake. The shop steward was prepared to stand up and be counted for his support for what management was doing when he thought it was doing right for the workers. The plant manager for his part was also adversely criticized. He was accused of 'conniving at workers' rule', of being a Communist (or a left-wing socialist). In fact he was neither. He was a disciplinarian, believing that discipline should be applied 'strictly and fairly', even to those who were helping him. He did in fact seek to persuade his men to work out a system of discipline for themselves, but in this he did not succeed.

Management encouraged the men to ask questions, and tried to answer them reasonably. Slowly, it became clear that there was to be no turning back. The plant manager had come to understand that 'you've got to believe in this sort of thing'. Deep within himself he had always known that the men were 'damned important' to the maintenance of the plant, 'much more important than machinery'. He had learned that it was wise to give a man a reason for asking him to do something. 'Just telling him to get on with it is not enough,' he said. When he gave an instruction for something difficult and tiring, he would say: 'When you've finished, nip down and have a shower and a cup of tea.' Why not be honest and fair, he asked himself, like a reasonable human being? 'You've got to think about the worker as a person,' he said. He added that it was nothing but common sense to have a little interest in the people who work for you. He said that it cost nothing in money, but that it cost a great deal of time. It was time, he thought, well spent. 'With this business,' he said hesitantly, 'there comes a point when you are getting into – dare I say it? – a religious premise.' In fact a state of justice and of consequent trust had been created. Even an element of love might have crept in, he said, again with diffidence. I agreed. Yet, of course, the justice and the trust had come first. Things were different now. When he went round the plant, men would look up at him and say 'Good morning, Mr C.'. 'It was very encouraging, and I enjoyed it,' he said. When the firm promoted him, and he was obliged to leave the plant, he was 'tremendously upset at going'. The men threatened to take industrial action if he was taken away from them. They were persuaded to take no action by a firm pledge from management that his policy would be carried on.

Both in this plant and in the cigarette factory, there had been no original declaration of management philosophy. There had scarcely been any philosophy at all, except for a firm recognition that the undertaking had to be made to pay, and for a sensitivity that made management feel that men's happiness mattered, and for a willingness to learn about them. In the course of time, in the school of experience, management developed a strangely unexpressed way of life, a style of management based upon a recognition of what must be done then and there. There was the will to see the human needs of the workers and to minister to them as they were perceived. At the cigarette factory there were sports grounds around the buildings. Once these had been football and cricket clubs for the workers. Now the workers preferred their sport in the vicinity of their homes and the sports grounds were let out to local clubs. The company proceeded existentially according to human apprehension of present human need. If this could be described as opportunist, there is no shame in rising to the opportunity to minister to need. Behind the opportunism lay managemental expertise and human capacity and willingness to learn. In the cigarette factory (and in the brewery) some of those in management were in fact dedicated men; this became obvious in time to those who worked for them.

We turn now to that style of leadership which, with high and sincere idealism, proclaims a 'philosophy of management'. A company with a deservedly good reputation for its industrial relationships issues a *Charter for Human Relations*. In this charter, the company declares that 'one of its most important responsibilities is to create a working environment in which its employees can happily perform their daily duties'. The charter asserts the respect due to all individual workers. It affirms their need for satisfaction in their work and promises the just reward due to them for their efforts and competence. The operations manager speaks with sincerity and conviction of the human dignity of the worker and with respect for the good work done by most of the employees. He goes on to mention the necessary 'element of manipulation' in managemental relationships with workers. The Scottish manager and the cigarette firm managemental team might have jibbed at this term (and at the thought behind it). It implied no ill will, but it seemed to deny that absolute trust which the Scottish manager at least had asked of himself and of others. In a later chapter we shall see how research has proved that trustfulness and trustworthiness are not mere beautiful ideals but necessary pre-conditions of good industrial relationship. Cynics (or 'hard-faced business men') may sneer, and yet they might find that trust sometimes works, that the production lines move on, the men that keep them moving keep themselves working, and all without manipulation.

Near Glasgow, at Tannoy's Coatbridge factory, loudspeakers and hi-fi equipment are made. There is a 'Work Improvement Project' there, which aims to improve the quality of working life by creating a collaborative process between management and workers to deal with difficulties before they become grievances. It seeks to make the best use of the skills and abilities of all employed. The basic unit of the system is the 'work group'. There are ten such groups of workers, each one comprising about fifteen persons working together. In addition, there is a 'management work group' and a work group for the administrative staff. Each of these groups nominally meets fortnightly. The work group meetings encourage a high level of communication among the members; they represent the grass roots of participation. The work groups each elect a representative, and these representatives, together with those of management meet monthly with the union convener and the district secretary of the union. They constitute the 'Work Improvement Committee', which is chaired successively by representatives of management and of labour. Each in turn holds the chair for a six-month period. I was privileged to be allowed to attend a Work Improvement Committee meeting. Ideas ventilated in the work groups come up to the Work Improvement Committee. Sometimes they become policy. When finance is involved, it may be necessary for management to reject them, especially as the company is the subsidiary of an American company. The General Manager says: 'If we disapprove of something very strongly we will veto it. The management might even veto a suggestion that does not involve extra expenditure. I think it is most important to say this clearly. Managers must not pretend that they give an idea any further consideration when they know full well that they are not even going to entertain it.'[13] That is honest, like everything else about him. The atmosphere in the Work Improvement Committee seemed a little tired, a little strained. The District Secretary of the union, the Managerial Administrative Technical and Supervisory Association (MATSA), the staff section of the GMWU, to which all employees belong, told me that the committee provides an opportunity for workers' representatives to talk to management and to be listened to. He believes that many irritations have been made to disappear through the group structure, and that workers have seen many group meeting suggestions accepted and implemented. 'It allows communication upward and downwards,' he says. Mrs Mary Weir, an Honorary Fellow of the University of Glasgow, seconded from the Work Research Unit of the Department of Employment, monitors the whole project. The General Manager described her to me as 'a catalyst and an arbitrator, gingering people up if enthusiasm flags and perhaps helping to avert any major disagreements'. She calls herself 'a prop and a plodder'. She spends two days a week at Coatbridge, stimulating management, work groups, individuals. She is mature and realistic enough to realize the significant role which she plays at Tannoy. Behind her is this dedicated General Manager, himself able at times to speak to the whole work force of 200. He is a man who in a previous post has seen with pain the dereliction caused by insecurity of employment, a man utterly determined to maintain security of employment for his workers in his present post.

At Coatbridge, there are only three production supervisors for 150 workers on the floor; there are two other supervisors (for production supply and for stores). There are no inspectors. Tannoy encourages its workers to accept responsibility by inspecting their own work. The sound testing of their products has become one part of the duty of the work groups. The atmosphere at Coatbridge is both industrious and relaxed – it is one of fellowship. The factory is small and the number of workers is small. I looked at it all with admiration, but wondered whether there was not too much managemental philosophy and design and not enough workers' say in that philosophy and design. An equally sincere but more tentative moving forward, with a finger on the pulse of the work force, with sensitivity for its state of mind, for what it was able to take, might have been more fulfilling for all. Growth cannot be from above. Pace is limited by capacity.

We are beginning to see that where there is the best of management there has to be that humility which seeks to make it even better, that non-paternalism which recognizes that workers sometimes know better than management what is best for them. We have already reached the point where it is obvious that part of the respect due to people consists in encouraging them to share in the very business of management itself. This involves risks, but the history of British industry since the Industrial Revolution has been a history of risk-taking which has been richly rewarded.

5 The Shop Steward

Although only about 12 million, out of a total working population of about 26 million, are unionized, it might be fair to say that the typical industrial worker is a union man (or woman) and that his chosen representative is the shop steward. For the purpose of industrial relations the shop steward is a key man. For those who do not care for him or for the union which elected him to his office he will not go away. He is here to stay, and those who care for the welfare of industry need to look at him fairly and squarely, prepared to learn something about him.

He is the trade unionist most frequently brought before the public on the television and in the other news media. He is the person most misrepresented by the news media and most misunderstood by that large section of the public dependent upon the news media for its knowledge of industry. Even responsible media sometimes convey prejudiced statements concerning him. Number 6 of the (Christian) *Audenshaw Papers*, for example, published in February 1979, includes the following: 'There has, of course, been a major shift of power towards the unions and especially to union shop stewards.' The writer goes on: 'A very small number of workers can paralyse economic production and cause great inconvenience to their fellow citizens.' This kind of writing seems to imply that shop stewards are wont to use their power for purposes of disruption. 'It's always the shop stewards who are at the root of the trouble at British Leyland,' said an angry but intelligent young man to the Oxford Young Conservatives on 14 November 1979. He spoke, he said, from special knowledge of BL. He was, however, not actually employed there, and many of those who are employed there would disagree with him. It is tragic that in the minds of many who know nothing of industry the phrase 'shop steward' should have become synonymous with wrecking and work-shy tendencies. For this unjust representation of the shop steward, prejudiced or ignorant comments by the news media are at least partially to blame.

It would be enlightening for persons quite ignorant of trade unionism in industry to read the Transport and General Workers' Union *Shop Stewards Handbook* on 'Relations with Management: 'Settle your grievances . . . whenever possible . . . The workers' strength does not lie in lung power, it lies in a good case, skilfully presented, backed by solid organization. With these things the workers can be confident that they can get what they want by normal negotiation . . . The workers rightly demand a respected status in industry, and courtesy and considerate treatment. The obligation works both ways. The workers should themselves show the courtesy to the management which they hope to receive.' This is what the largest of the unions expects of its shop stewards. Let us try to reduce that prejudice against shop stewards felt by many outside industry who are quite ignorant of their work and duties.

In *Work Place Industrial Relations 1972*, a social survey carried out on behalf of the Department of Employment, Stanley Parker declared that a large majority of senior managers questioned believe that shop stewards, far from being trouble-makers, in fact help in the solution of industrial problems.[1] More than half of the senior managers, Mr Parker found, believe that shop stewards assist with production. Derek Robinson, a communist, formerly chairman of the Leyland Combine Trade Union Committee, and also the senior trade union representative on the Leyland Cars' Joint Management Council, publicly declared in 1978 that the shop stewards had with management the common aim of securing a profitable future for the company.[2] His chief point of difference at that time from his company chairman, Sir Michael Edwardes, was that he thought that the company ought to aim at production of a million vehicles, while Sir Michael believed that only 819,000 could be sold. Derek Robinson publicly pledged the support of the BL shop stewards for BL management in its declared intention to 'achieve a much higher United Kingdom market share than any of our uninformed critics believe possible'. This was in 1978, before very serious differences developed. It is not well remembered. In Report 17 for the Donovan Commission (*Facilities Afforded to Shop Stewards*), G. Woodcock, I. T. Blakeman and J. N. Edwards stated: 'We have found little evidence that the steward is innately hostile to management, and much evidence that his lack of co-operation, where it exists, can sometimes be explained by management's failure to accept fully the steward's role.[3] They recommend management to recognize the effective part which shop stewards can play in maintaining and improving effective industrial relationships.

We have already seen in chapter 4 how a Scottish senior shop steward, a truck driver, proved an incomparable ally to his manager in the whole task of improving conditions of work in a plant. Dr Alan Fox, the distinguished Oxford sociologist, an authority on trade union history, industrial relations and the wider issues of industrial society, writes: 'Research shows shop stewards in fact acting more as a lubricant than an irritant: as being more often supporters of order, exercising a restraining influence, than otherwise; and as only rarely finding themselves involved in strikes or other forms of industrial action.'[4] As a matter of fact, the average shop steward is a hard-working man, often elected by his fellow workers in preference to the communist (or Trotskyist) candidate, carrying the unrewarded burden of stewardship with dignity and responsibility. Jack Burton, a somewhat unusual bus driver, describes his position as branch chairman for two years of his union, as he passed endlessly from individual to committee to management, apparently satisfying no one and abused by all. He could not have a cup of tea in the canteen or walk to work without being approached by someone about something. He felt intensely lonely. 'When I walked into the canteen this morning before starting my shift, no less than four people approached me . . . I wanted to speak to my conductor, but couldn't reach him!'[5] Shop stewards are usually treated by management as the proper representatives of the workers with whom to consult, bargain and negotiate. Often they are men (and women) of outstanding character and leadership capacity, whose co-operation if secured is of great value to the industry in which they serve. The shop steward's role and significance have in fact been described in many books and in countless articles in industrial relations periodicals. No one wise or with any real knowledge seeks to denigrate the vital importance to industry of the shop steward.

The Donovan Commission, containing representatives of management as well as of unions, unanimously referred to the 'important services' of shop stewards. It described shop stewards as 'rarely agitators pushing workers towards unconstitutional action'. Rather, it goes on, they are 'quite commonly . . . supporters of order, exercising a restraining influence upon their members'. It referred to shop stewards in the motor-industry, who 'like shop stewards elsewhere, are in general hard-working and responsible people who are making a sincere effort to do a difficult job'.[6] That difficult job is primarily to look after the interests of those who elect them. The bulk of a shop steward's work lies in 'grievance-handling'. Men who have elected him bring to the steward their often legitimate grievances (which may be due to no one's fault, but to the inevitable failure of various persons to foresee everything). There is no sin in having a grievance; it is a technical term for cause for complaint. The complaint itself may be amicably made and amicably settled. Again and again, shop stewards say, they have to sort the grievances out, sometimes taking them to management, sometimes refusing to do so. The job calls for wisdom; and while many do not care to accept the inevitable burden involved, those who allow themselves to be nominated are normally men who are prepared conscientiously to stand up for those who have chosen them, in so far as they have a reasonable case to put forward. A good shop steward will sometimes have to consult his senior shop steward or the convener, sometimes the district officer of his union. 'If any of your members has an individual grievance or a problem, you have the responsibility to see you do your best to help him,' says the TGWU *Shop Stewards Handbook*. An Electrical Electronic Telecommunication and Plumbing Union (EETPU) shop steward speaks with respect of a steward of another union who is well known for his Trotskyist tendencies, one thoroughly out of favour with his own union locally. Yet, says the EETPU man, he has won the 'veneration' of his own constituency who will not have a word spoken against him, because his men know how well he looks after the interests of each of them.

This is reality which has to be recognized. A middle-aged Irish Catholic, a family man working in the same plant, says of this truck driver shop steward: 'I'd put my life down for him. He's a genuine person, he's for the working man.' He says that 'he has it all worked out what he's going to say'. 'He's too clever for them,' he adds. Yet all this contrasts with the experience of the young Oxford 'trucker' who told me that he had been several days in the paint shop before someone pointed out his shop steward to him.

Naturally, a keen shop steward seeks not only to defend his members' rights but to seek better conditions for them. Management tends too often (but not always) to wait until this seeking takes place to grant those better conditions. If there were more unsolicited giving, there would be less unscrupulous taking. 'My job,' says John Power, the senior shop steward and convener, 'is to improve my members' living standards.'

My friend, Ron Powell, formerly a maintenance electrician at British Leyland's Speke No. 2 plant on Merseyside, describes his shop floor impression of the shop steward. If an operator has a problem, he says, 'his only line of communication is through his foreman, and if that foreman is indifferent to the man's needs, then his only other outlet is a complaint to his shop steward who will not be indifferent and will know how to cut corners and get things done'.[7] Gradually, he adds, the shop steward becomes the 'focal point' on the shop floor. This is unsolicited praise from a skilled worker of experience, integrity and honesty. Simon Fraser, formerly Secretary of the Trades Council of Liverpool, describes the shop steward to me as 'an astute man, elected for his negotiating ability'. He is a treaty-making man, rather than a treaty-breaking man.

The shop steward is not *ipso facto* a firebrand. He is in fact a pivotal man in British industry. He has been around (but not in the pages of the press or on television) for a long time. He is no post-war phenomenon. The shop steward, or the 'father of the chapel' (as he is called in some of the craft unions) has long played a behind-the-scenes part in British industry. The 'chapel' itself seems to date back to the eighteenth century (or earlier), when a senior compositor acted as president of the compositors of a workshop and was known as 'father of the chapel'.[8] As long ago as 1824 'shop stewards' collected dues in the Foundry Workers' Union.[9] In the Amalgamated Society of Engineers, shop stewards were receiving complaints and referring back to the District Committees in 1892.[10] A shop stewards' movement originated on the Clyde in 1915. J. Hinton writes: 'The shop stewards' movement was a child of war . . . The shop stewards' movement developed out of a situation in which the alienation of trade union leadership from the rank and file under the impact of national collective bargaining was greatly intensified by the collaboration of the trade union executives in the war effort. Consequently the rank and file had to construct their own defences, independently of their officials.'[11] The shop steward was the instrument of, perhaps the originator of, a rank-and-file movement which after two wars has moved power in the unions from the centre to the shop floor. If this is not liked, it is a fact which has to be accepted. At least here on the shop floor are not faceless officials but men (and women) who are to be seen at their benches or on the assembly line day by day. The Donovan Commission (of 1968) estimated that there were at that time probably about 175,000 stewards in the country, compared with perhaps 3000 full-time trade union officers.[12] Alan Fox, writing in 1978, reckons that the number of shop stewards in British industry has risen to 300,000.[13]

The Donovan Commission stated that 'without shop stewards, trade unions would lack for members, for money, and for means of keeping in touch with their members'.[14] The TGWU *Shop Stewards Handbook* says that the steward is the 'representative of the union', carrying in trust 'a responsibility for an organization which has taken generations of struggle and service to build up'. He has to pay intelligent regard to the policy of the Union, it tells him, and he is to do his best to see that this is carried out. He is to recruit new members, keep existing members up to scratch and turn card holders into trade unionists. 'The Steward,' says the EETPU *Shop Stewards Handbook*, 'is the vital link in the structure of the Union. More than any other Union official it is the Steward who makes the Union live, in the plant and on the shop floor.' It counsels the steward that 'every new employee should be approached as soon as possible and encouraged to join the union'. It tells the steward that 'the average Union member does not personally know the Full-time Officials of the Union'. It says to him: 'You are the Union.' It tells him that he is to try, with the co-operation of other members, to make the shop 'a 100% union shop'. Employers may not care for such enthusiasm; but there is nothing sinister about it.

The Donovan Commission made it clear that 'the most important of the British shop steward's tasks' is 'the service which he performs by helping to regulate workers' pay and working conditions and by representing them in dealings with management'.[15] It cannot be over-emphasized that shop stewards are not normally revolutionary-minded upstarts chosen by groups of discontented workers, but the official, recognized representatives of the industrial work force, to whom management is quite properly obliged to grant time for the performing of their recognized functions as stewards. 'Since April 1, 1978, when the time off provisions of the Employment Protection Act 1975 came into force, employers have been statutorily required to give time off with pay to their shop stewards to enable them to carry out their industrial relations duties.'[16] Nor is the shop steward's recognized function on the shop floor merely the result of Labour Governments' legislation in the 1970s. In the 'Blue Book' of the Ford Motor Company, dated 1977, the earlier agreement of 25 July 1969 is re-published. It states that: 'The Company recognizes the right of the Employees to have an adequate number of representatives appointed on a craft, departmental or geographical basis to act on their behalf.' It goes on to say that 'the representatives shall be known as Shop Stewards', and that 'the appointment of such Shop Stewards shall be determined by the Unions concerned'. It stipulates, not unreasonably, that those appointed shall have fulfilled at least one year's service with the company. The names of those elected to office as shop stewards are to be notified in writing by the union to the company; and the company guarantees 'reasonable facilities' to the shop stewards for carrying out their duties. According to the 'Blue Book', the shop steward may leave the area for which he is appointed 'in pursuance of Union duties with the written permission of his Superintendent or Foreman . . . such permission not to be unreasonably withheld'. Provision is made for a substitute to act for the shop steward in the event of his illness. Actions taken by shop stewards 'in good faith in pursuance of their duties', the agreement says, 'shall not in any way affect their involvement with the Company'.

The shop steward, elected to union office by the members on the shop floor, is by no means in trade union theory independent of the national organization of that union. In the Amalgamated Union of Engineering Workers (AUEW) *Shop Stewards Manual*, the steward is told that he has not only been elected by AUEW members in his particular shop but that the Union's District Committee has approved the election (after checking that he has been an adult member for at least twelve months). The steward carries a credential card issued by the District Secretary. 'All Shop Stewards are under the control of the District Committee,' says the *Manual*, and none may function until the District Committee approval is given. The TGWU shop stewards are told in their *Handbook*: 'In dealing with many of your problems the Union will expect you to manage on your own. If you cannot, you know you have the power and resources of the TGWU behind you . . . Sooner or later . . . even the strongest workshop group needs help from fellow workers outside. It is, therefore, a matter of self-interest not to undermine the unity of the working class which is expressed in the trade union movement.' The AUEW in its *Rules* reminds its members that 'in the case of a shop steward they shall not leave their employment without the approval of the District Committee'. In the AUEW the District Committee is indeed powerful; but even in the TGWU the *Handbook* instructs the shop steward to tell the District Officer in advance whenever anything is likely to happen which might conflict with union policy or have repercussions outside the work place.

In practice, the books issued by the unions are intended to be general guides rather than binding legislation, a union organizer tells me. 'What actually happens, how stringently the rules are kept (or how casually they are ignored), depends upon the history and tradition of unionism in the place of work,' says Roger Sealey, a BL shop steward in Oxford. Where there is no local full-time official, shop stewards tend inevitably to be more independent. In the EETPU, for example, Oxford shop stewards know that the area official is thirty miles away. They feel, rightly or wrongly, that he is 'out of touch', that he 'doesn't deal with reality'. Yet his *Shop Stewards Handbook* reminds the EETPU steward that he 'has no power to sanction strike action of his own accord'. It goes on: 'Disputes of this seriousness must be reported immediately to the Area Official.'

A picture is emerging of a relationship between the shop steward and the full-time official of the union which inevitably depends to some extent upon personalities, but also upon the industrial experience of full-time officials, and upon local tradition. The relationship is normally close, and the keen shop steward is usually a keen union man, prepared to look beyond his own limited constituency. The full-time official is often a former shop steward, with intimate understanding of the job of the man on the shop floor. Messrs Batstone, Boraston and Frenkel, referring to a major manufacturing plant, say that 'most full-time officials, at least in the manual unions, have themselves been conveners and understand the need for steward leadership and organizational unity'.[17] The AUEW District Committee normally takes care to elect a local man with experience of local industry. He must have lived in the district for at least a year. Frequently he is a former senior shop steward who has been persuaded to accept nomination. In problems arising between a shop steward and his senior shop steward, at least one full-time official, a friend of mine, makes it a rule not to see the former except in the presence of the latter. *Research Paper 10* for the Donovan Commission reports that 'nearly all the full-time officers interviewed were enthusiastic about the work of stewards'.[18]

The elected shop steward may be a dull but worthy fellow, probably trustworthy but maybe uninspiring. On the other hand he may be what Huw Beynon, the Durham University sociologist, describes as 'very bright, very sharp . . . a charismatic leader',[19] a man (or woman) full of intellectual power, energy, vitality. If he could be persuaded to 'cross the frontier', he could rise high in management. His mental calibre is of top management quality. But, for reasons which we shall consider in chapter 8, he is not likely to be persuaded to change sides. He has made his choice: to be a union man. In his union he may become a senior shop steward, or even a convener, in his twenties. After that there is nothing, unless he becomes a full-time union official, goes over to management or leaves industry. He may well become frustrated, unfulfilled. His trouble is probably no fault of his own; often, in part at least, it is his lack of education. John Power, for fourteen years (and more) a senior shop steward at Cowley, and in 1979 a candidate who polled well at the General Election, declared himself to me 'a half-educated storeman'. Consciously or unconsciously, the shop steward is usually in need of further education. The average shop steward suffers, and knows that he suffers, from that education in English schools which is for those who do not aspire to O-levels and A-levels. Yet it is possible for young men and women to develop and satisfy a thirst for education after school, if the kind of education they need is made available for them and if they manage to catch some sort of vision of its potentiality. Thus training, and especially the right kind of training, is important for shop stewards if they are to do their jobs well and responsibly, and if they are to find their lives satisfying as shop stewards.

It is common for a person to begin office as a steward without any knowledge of the job or any training for it. A man elected at Scott Bader's at Wollaston confessed to his manager: 'I'm damned if I know what to do.' Scott Bader's is no common firm. They sent him (in a company car) to a residential TUC shop stewards' course at Birmingham. In addition to residential courses, there are also day-release courses run by the TUC. A personal friend, a mature shop steward in his fifties, is doing a weekly day-release course at this time of writing. He is a well-read man, a Methodist lay preacher, and he is enjoying every minute of this TUC course. The TUC has its one-day courses and its week-end schools. Courses are given on behalf of the TUC on industry and on particular industries, at Polytechnics and Technical Colleges, at Colleges of

Further Education and Colleges of Technology. At Oxford the Department of External Studies provides the teachers for the courses, the employers provide the finance, the unions decide who shall go on them, and the department and the unions jointly draw up the curriculum. The TUC runs some seventy correspondence courses, and courses are organized for the TUC by the Workers' Educational Association as well as by the external and extra-mural departments of universities.

Courses are also organized by particular unions. There are residential courses for GMWU and EETPU stewards in their own union colleges. The GMWU runs its shop stewards' courses (lasting four and a half days) at Woodstock Hall. The EETPU tells its shop stewards in their *Handbook*: 'The Union's own College at Esher has therefore consistently striven to provide shop stewards with short term courses aimed at training them in the techniques of industrial relations practice and providing them with insight and knowledge into the problems of their own and other industries.' It warns stewards to ensure that in the matter of day release for training the union 'is fully consulted over the choice of syllabus and selection of tutors'. The union 'is responsible for the selection of students'. There are also company-organized courses for shop stewards. John Power is sceptical concerning these, claiming that they are 'company-conditioned'.

Sometimes a devoted shop steward cannot find the time for courses held outside working hours. 'My husband is always on the telephone,' says a shop steward's wife. The husband is a man of conscience, anxious to do all he can for his fellow electricians, his constituency. Also he has three children, and his wife works part-time. Not for him, therefore, residential or week-end courses. However, under the Employment Protection Act of 1975, employees who are officials of their unions are allowed 'time off' for industrial relations training approved by the TUC or by their union, and without loss of earnings. Opportunity opens up.

The training courses provided by the TUC and the unions are practical. They tend to deal with the steward's role, with grievances, safety, communications, negotiations, procedure agreements, unfair dismissals, codes of practice, union principles. On TUC one-day courses there is likely to be a session on 'industrial democracy'. Training is indeed needed in all these important matters. Yet there seems to be a lack of imaginativeness, of depth of treatment. Some of the men (and women) on the courses are people of intellectual capacity, capable indeed of tertiary education. One looks in vain for an attempt to give serious attention to the behavioural sciences. The shop steward may not only have to deal with the supervisor, with line management, but also with exasperated men inclined to 'wild-cat' action. What makes them like that? 'Don't bait the foreman,' says the TGWU *Shop Stewards Handbook*. The steward ought to know something about the working of foremen's and workers' minds, in addition to what he learns from (sometimes bitter) experience. He ought to learn something about the reasons for normal mental reactions, about the possibilities of unlikely reactions. What does one look for, how can one be helped to understand? 'Tom' meets his plant manager once a month; they always have a row. Why? Neither man is a fire-brand. Could the row somehow be avoided? Bruce Partridge writes in the *Industrial Relations Journal* that 'training is overly concerned with knowledge rather than behaviour'. He speaks of 'the inappropriateness of traditional steward training'.[20] No teacher would be wise to enter into relationships with children without some elementary basic training in the psychology of the child. Men in relationship with one another need to learn something of the minds of men.

A TGWU District Officer spoke to me with great respect of a steward who had difficulty in reading. He went on a shop stewards' course, lost confidence in himself and came away from it, saying: 'I'm no bloody good.' The full-time official said of him: 'He came out of the poverty of the Scottish coal fields. He was the finest shop steward I ever met. He was first-class by sheer basic instinct.' He went on to say wisely that there are people whom the environment makes, who need no learning. Such an exception does not invalidate the need for the training of the majority. More will be said of this need (and the answer to it) in chapter 10.

In Research Paper No. 10 for the Donovan Commission, W. E. J. McCarthy and S. R. Parker comment that some shop stewards function as scarcely more than channels for the objectives and strategies of others. Some, however, they say, 'provide a charismatic form of influence'.[21] For the benefit chiefly of those who have no personal knowledge of shop stewards, let us look hard now at four shop stewards, three non-militants and one militant, all of them men who have ably fulfilled their office. (I should add that even these four would have benefited from further opportunities for education stimulating to their keen and active minds.)

John, as I shall call him, is a prominent and highly respected

senior shop steward in his plant at Oxford, a keen TGWU man.
He believes himself to be one of a minority of 'real trade
unionists'. The majority, he adds, just belong. He came (like
many others) from a trade union family. At first he was in the
AUEW, then he transferred to the TGWU, because the shop
where he worked was TGWU. He was at once elected shop
steward. He has a sense of genuine camaraderie with his fellow
unionists. He also feels a 'camaraderie to a degree' with some
members of management; but, he says, 'comradeship depends
upon situations'. He is 'definitely friendly' with his plant manager.
Both have Christian sympathies. He is even prepared to trust
management 'to a degree'. He reckons that he can assess people,
but he adds that you must know people if you are to assess them.
Once you get to know people, he says, 'friendship comes'. Even
so, he would not make a habit of mixing socially with management. He would not drink with management, for example. He
knows that his men are suspicious, and he himself must be careful.
He would not, of course, address any member of management as
'Sir'. He cannot use the word, nor can he call anyone 'Mister'.
He says that management recognizes that that is his way, and that
is all right. He uses the Christian name to all management, including top management on the rare occasions that he sees it. He
has been offered promotion several times, but he has emphatically
refused it. He adds that he dissuades other trade unionists from
accepting it. Anyhow, he would not care to sit behind a desk – he
is frankly doubtful about the real authority of those who sit behind
desks. Yet he is no rebel. He accepts that there must be desks
and men behind them. He strongly wants to make his firm succeed. He even feels that a sense of dedication may be developing
in the workers. 'The change is coming,' he says. Here, in John,
is trade unionism at its most typical: canny, shrewd, willing to be
harnessed to the common cause, provided that he can see, know
and sum up management. He is even prepared to give trust to
management when he can see that management deserves it.

   In Oxford too lives Tom. Tom is not a militant, 'emphatically
not a militant,' he laughs to me. He is a Labour Party man, a
'moderate'. He recently allowed himself to be nominated for the
chairmanship of the local branch of his party, but he was not
elected. He was chosen two years ago as a shop steward by sixteen
of his fellow workers. He had previously been (for four years) a
senior shop steward in a smaller firm in the same town. In his
present (larger) firm he was recently re-elected to office. He does

not care for pressure groups such as the Socialist Workers Party, and he believes that the influence of the small minority of Trotskyist shop stewards is grossly exaggerated in the local press and in uninformed public opinion. He has a much higher respect for the few communist shop stewards. He is thirty-one, and he, too, comes from a union family.

When he was first elected a shop steward, he recognized that he was 'pretty naïve', and tried to remedy this. He took a weekend course with the University Department of External Studies, then a TUC postal course, and after that he attended a school at Cirencester organized by his union. He had two years at Ruskin College, Oxford, on a bursary provided for his first year by the TUC and for his second year by the TGWU, his union. He appreciated the time spent there and the quality of the tutors, but he feels that it is impossible for academics (or anyone else from outside industry) to understand industrial relations. At Ruskin he benefited from tertiary education, without allowing it to separate him from those of his own background and the men with whom he works. Tom has learnt a great deal, and is prepared to learn more.

Tom is not favourably impressed with management as he encounters it. Time was, they tell him, ten years ago or more, when the works manager would walk round the shop floor. Now even his plant manager does not appear on the floor (and would not be welcome there). Workers would not want him to interfere. He would not be technically qualified to do so, although Tom recognizes that technical qualification is not strictly necessary. Tom knows that the plant manager gets a regular feedback of information from his line-supervisors. By looking up papers he can know what is going on. His office, in fact, is quite close to the shop floor. Tom speaks to him regularly on the telephone, he tells me. The manager recognizes Tom's voice, and they are on Christian name terms. Tom does not think that the manager likes him. 'We don't hit it off personally,' he says. They only meet once a month, when there is a 'consultative meeting'. This is a conference of seven elected shop stewards with the departmental head and the superintendents. Tom is the chairman of the departmental shop stewards' committee which prepares the agenda a week before the meeting. He believes that the departmental head thinks him responsible for the controversial nature of the agendas. The meetings themselves are acrimonious. Decisions are not normally made at them, because the manager must always 'consult industrial relations'. Sometimes 'industrial relations' are represented at the monthly meetings, sometimes not.

Tom does not have a high opinion of 'industrial relations' in the works. By this, of course, he means the department. In fact he thinks that industrial relations departments are not useful at all. He believes that they tend to take the side of management, because they are management-employed, responsible to management. He thinks that the 'industrial relations people' are insensitive to what people on the shop floor feel. Finally, he believes strongly that they come between management and the workers. Management, he says, ought to be able to make decisions without them. 'In industrial relations,' he says, 'you need to deal with authority.' The necessity for management to consult 'industrial relations' prevents management from being the 'determining authority' whom the workers want to meet. 'Industrial relations' are a barrier, in Tom's mind, to good industrial relationships.

Tom wants us to be quite clear that he is not an agitator; he does not find any particular pleasure in complaining. Nevertheless, when asked, he gives a straightforward and reasoned opinion. He is not impressed with the supervisory staff. Sometimes, he says, the foreman cannot give an answer to a question. 'See the senior foreman,' he says. So the shop steward is sent to look for help elsewhere. Sometimes, says Tom, the foreman simply does not want to know. He adds that he himself would never, if asked, take a foreman's job. He believes that the foreman's position is undermined from both sides. Neither management nor the hourly-paid worker has confidence in him. As a result, the foreman simply does not care to get involved. He shrugs off responsibility. Last year, Tom says, there was a foremen's strike for two days. The plant got on fine without them. The shop stewards saw to it that productivity increased in their absence. Tom believes that the whole superintendent–senior foreman–foreman structure of line management could be dispensed with. Already, he says, it is the shop stewards who see to it that there is a fair allocation of overtime and lay-offs. If the foreman does not like what the shop stewards have done, the stewards go at once to the senior foreman or to the superintendent. The superintendents, he says, sometimes identify problems, but he believes that the settlement of them has in the end to be at a lower level. He is airing views of great significance which deserve to be thought about. To what extent, when and where, can shop stewards take over from foremen, and with what effectiveness?

The company, under relatively new management, is proud of its communications. Tom declares that the communications system does not extend to him or his work-mates. 'Communications,' he says, 'are non-existent.' He reports that the invariable answer to reasonable requests for information is that none is available. Management, he tells me, does not bother to answer questions. Tom thinks that management believes that if it gives information it loses power. 'It becomes more vulnerable.' 'So you ask the toilet cleaner,' he says. 'He probably knows.' Maybe Tom is not being fair to management. Yet Tom does try to be fair. He is no fool; this is how he feels; this is what seems to him to happen.

In Tom's plant there are no strikes. However, Tom admits that there are stoppages, which sometimes last several days. They are unofficial, in the sense that they are not given formal or financial support by the union. However, he believes that the union's local organizer knows about them and is 'probably involved'. Tom has no doubt that it is on the shop floor that the union is most truly to be found. Where there is a stoppage, it is often the men on the floor rather than the shop steward who initiate it. 'They just tell the shop steward that under these circumstances they will not work.' That is all there is to it. The local paper probably gives the shop stewards the blame. They may well not have earned it.

Tom himself believes strongly that it is just not possible at present to improve relationships, because the employer cannot offer the job security which the men require. He says that, above all else, the workers want to remain where they are, where their homes are, and with their jobs guaranteed to them. Management, on the other hand, needs a mobile labour force, needs to have workers who can be moved as required, moved where they are most needed or dispensed with if they are needed no longer. Tom knows his fellow workers. They have grown up together in the same part of Oxford. He knows that they want to work on and live on in the environment they are used to. Some have not travelled much further than Abingdon; one worker's wife hopes one day to see Swindon and shop there (although her children have been to Wales). People are Oxford-born and Oxford-bred. They want to stay there, and that is all there is to it. Insulation against job insecurity is what the worker wants, Tom says. He feels that management does not realize this. Management has a different tradition, not the same needs, and anyway, may not be able to afford to guarantee jobs. Indeed management may not care at all for Tom's views. They must, however, be taken seriously. They are the considered views of an educated and thoughtful young man, who thinks of himself as just one of the silent majority – an opinion which is probably correct.

We turn from Tom to Geoff, also a young shop steward working for the same car manufacturing firm, but in a different plant. Geoff went to work when he was sixteen, direct from a grammar school. He regrets that he did not stay at school long enough to take his O-levels. He has taken some educational courses at the College of Further Education, but has had no shop steward training. He is well-spoken, quiet, relaxed. He was happy to be elected a shop steward, and is glad to have the opportunity of representing his fellow-workers. He has been a shop steward for four years. He joined the communist party after his initial election claims that some who elected him were not aware that he was a communist. Anyhow, he has been re-elected to office. He has recently left the party but he is still 'a supporter'. 'This does not imply any great change in my opinions,' he says. He believed when he was elected, and he still believes, that his prime duty is to speak up for those who elected him, whenever need arises. He tells me that he deplores the manipulation of workers for political reasons by International Socialists. He speaks well of some of the foremen; but he feels a certain pity for them because of their eroded status. On the other hand, he doubts whether the plant could do without supervisory authority. With his fellow shop stewards, he has access to the plant manager, when approaches to the foremen and to the superintendent have not produced results. He says that his plant manager does not cross the shop floor. He adds that the manager's presence on the floor would arouse suspicion. Again and again, we come across this extraordinary absence of management from the shop floor.

Geoff believes that there is considerable distrust of management. This dates, he thinks from the days when the company was independent. Now that it is nationalized, he hopes that the workers will come to trust management. However, as time goes on, he becomes less hopeful. He feels strongly that, if hourly-paid workers were trusted more, they would respond. He says, for example, that if clocking-in were abolished the workers themselves would deal adequately with those who were late for work. They would not allow themselves to be let down. He thinks that the office staff is favoured in this respect, since more trust is obviously placed in them than in the hourly-paid workers. He believes that management must learn to entrust the shop stewards with more information. There is a feeling, he says, that 'no one will tell you'. If men are to be genuinely involved, they must have greater access to information. He adds, mildly enough, that they must also have more say in the making of decisions. He suggests that they feel frustrated when their opinions are asked but the ultimate decisions are reserved to management. This, he says, is a relic of the old class system, in which management seemed to have a 'natural' superiority over its work-force. He believes that this class-consciousness is passing away. He knows that, at least in a nationalized company, the profit motive should no longer dominate. He believes in the importance of incentives, to show men clearly that it is in their own interest to work hard. He says all this softly and thoughtfully.

For himself he seeks an adequate and decent wage. This is not quite according to the principle of 'from each according to his ability, to each according to his needs'. However, it seems reasonable enough. Geoff does not pretend to know what is happening in the Soviet Union and of how things are done there. The sadness is that this reasonable, sensible, decent young near-communist is losing some of his hopefulness. It is interesting (and ought to be noted by all who assume communists to be wreckers of industrial relations) that Jack Keiser and Kevin T. Kelly, in *Perspectives on Strikes*, report a case where 'we have been led by a prominent Communist and have not had one strike in five years'.[22] The car manufacturing firm could do with more shop stewards of Geoff's calibre, communist or no communist.

We move from Oxford to Liverpool, from John and Tom and Geoff to Eddie Roberts. That is his real name. He has already been vividly described in Huw Beynon's *Working for Ford*.[23] He is an activist, a militant, formerly a senior shop steward at Ford's, of Halewood, Liverpool. He was born in 1941 in a working-class area of Liverpool; at eleven he won a grammar school scholarship to the prestigious Liverpool Institute. He left school before taking public examinations, but his handwriting and his command of written English bear witness to the quality of his education. He worked at Dunlop's for four years, and then at Ford's from 1962 until 1970. He became a Ford's shop steward in 1963, after telling his wife that 'the place is a bloody madhouse' and that he would either see some changes or get the sack. He uses invective freely of friend and foe, in the Merseyside style. He is a family man, with two children, proud of his dependence on Carol his wife in the midst of constant industrial warfare. He works by day and night, takes his children to the pictures and sleeps through the programme. So his wife tells me. He legitimately calls himself a civilized man, believing with heart and soul in civilized relationships. He is appalled at the horror of industries which invade Liverpool, create dependence, and then move out to more profitable areas, expecting to leave behind them a market for their products. 'Why should they be allowed to exist?' he asks. For himself and his friends he asks for 'enough to pay the electricity bills'. There is a personal gentleness underlying his rough tongue. Now, in 1980, he feels the redundancies in Liverpool as if they were his own.

He became senior shop steward on night shift in the paint, trim and assembly plant at Ford's in 1966, and was selected TGWU convener there in 1968. He was chosen for the National Joint Negotiating Board of Ford's in 1969. As a shop steward he came to know his fellow workers; he knew them pastorally, knew where they lived, knew many of their homes. He knows them now (and their children). He was prepared to fight the battles of those whom he represented. However, he 'certainly didn't want to see his men running down the street spitting blood'. When he was at Ford's, he belonged to no political party. Yet he says that all his thinking was coloured by Ford's. Ford's made him what he is, he claims. He was prepared, he says, to work with management. He avoided many a confrontation, and was ready to work reasonably with managers who were reasonable with him. He recalls how a reasonable manager allowed him to collect the union dues during working hours (in those distant days) instead of his having to collect them during the dinner hour. He says that this manager incurred both the jealousy of his fellow managers and the hostility of higher authority. He removed himself. He did not fit in, Eddie said. 'Ford managers are horrible people,' Eddie summed up. 'They hate one another.' He eventually became convinced that Ford's determination to maximize profits at all costs 'made civilized relationships impossible'.

A picture may be emerging of a man hopelessly prejudiced against his employers. This is not true of the Eddie Roberts whom many in Liverpool (and elsewhere) know. It was just that he had come to believe, rightly or wrongly, that he was up against an inhuman system with no care for human beings. Ford's was 'a well-oiled machine', he says, demanding 'an inhumanity which Ford's have always had'. He instances one occasion when, as a shop steward, he was sent for from the paint shop. There was a large, physical-culture-worshipping superintendent in charge. 'A bully boy,' Eddie called him, 'a cowboy.' The line had been accelerated, Eddie said. 'The paint was flying, there was vaseline and paint over everybody.' Eddie told the superintendent: 'The line's going too bloody fast. You're killing these men.' The superintendent told him that he did not care for shop stewards who came into his section. He told Eddie: 'There's nothing wrong with the spray. We've got no problems down here.' When Eddie had gone, the superintendent called all the men out and asked each one of them: 'What's your beef?' No one complained, Eddie said. The line raced on. Men wanted to keep their jobs.

In reaction to all this, Eddie's political consciousness was quickened. It was reaction 'to that employer and his iniquity'. He had in fact no party political affiliation during his time at Halewood. He only joined one (for a short period) after he had left Ford's and become a paid TGWU official. He sought integrity and devotion in politics, and failed to find it, so he came out. His bitter speaking against Ford's comes from a man of charm and warmth of friendship, of sensitivity and compassion. No doubt Ford's would reply ably to his charges. The tragedy remains that his innate capacity, his organizing ability, his gift for the leadership of a devoted following could not somehow have been used at Ford's for the common good. It is sad too that his experiences there should leave him, ten years after his departure from Ford's, with so little good to say for his former employers. No doubt there were faults on both sides. This able but brash young man had capacity for both dedication and exasperation. Ford's failure to bring out the best in him illustrates the comment of Lord Allen, of the Union of Shop, Distributive and Allied Workers (USDAW), to the effect that 'there is too much frustration and suspicion on the shop floor'. Lord Allen adds that it will take courageous management and the help of the unions to break it down. Eddie left Ford's in 1970 to become a full-time official of his union. He writes, however, that the picture is not wholly black. 'We are still primarily extended by the routine and generally peaceable activities of resolving wage-related matters; and the daily humour of our people alters little.'

Above are thumb-nail sketches of shop stewards as they are, of men with and without much education, but all men of considerable capacity. These are the kind of able men whom industrialists ought to try to learn to live and work with. They are men whose co-operation might be won by good management. They are men capable of sharing to some extent in management itself, if some way might be found of using them without asking them to leave their unions, to cross to the other side. We shall be considering in the remaining chapters the possibility of using such men and of using the unions themselves in co-operation with industrial management.

6 The Greeks Had a
Word for It

We have had a look at management and seen something of it in action, have seen it at its best in some places and seen something of its weaknesses in others. We have seen a little of that important union person, the shop steward, seen some of his capacities and some of his limitations. We are reaching a point where we may begin to think more deeply about what is wrong in industrial relations, before making positive suggestions about what should be done to put right what is wrong.

I started off in chapter 3 by suggesting strongly that for good industrial relations there must be respect for people whatever their jobs may be. I have also at least hinted that there must also be respect for those groupings in which people place themselves. John, of chapter 5, is a fine cheerful worker, a first-rate senior shop steward, on the best of terms with his plant manager. However, John is also a keen dedicated union man. To know and respect John for what he is ought to encourage knowledge of and respect for that union which he represents and which has helped to make him what he is. Take John with all his qualities (or leave him), but you cannot have him without accepting that union background and setting which is his, which has long been his and which is likely to remain his. What is needed is respect not only for John but for John's union too. It is easy to give John respect. But to the non-unionist the union is unknown, possibly communist-dominated and generally an object of suspicion. We can grow out of these attitudes.

Eric Jacobs, Assistant Editor of *The Sunday Times*, writing after the long shutdown of *The Times*, declares:

What I think is extraordinary is the high degree of identification that most of the staff showed with their union and the low degree of identification they felt with the company. You might never have thought that at the end of the day it was the company that paid the wages. It was the company that produced the newspapers, provided the jobs and indirectly created the union members. The fact was that the company had failed to enlist the loyalties of its staff. It had failed to convince them that they did have a common interest. I am not now talking about union militants but about ordinary union members, perhaps even many who were reluctant to join a union in the first place. Whoever they were and whatever their views, the company simply failed to make a significant purchase on their loyalties. . . It is this broad background, this general atmosphere of mistrust and misunderstanding, rather than any particular action by the company that seems to me to have been the most important cause of the long shutdown of Times Newspapers. And it is in this, I think, that the most important lesson lies for the other companies.[1]

The allegiance of the unionist to the union is hard for a non-union person to comprehend. It is none the less real. Jim Hughes, Director and General Manager of Tannoy, writes from Coatbridge of a former convener that he is 'a committed unionist'. This he accepts and he commends ('a view which I would share'). It seems a pity that CBI National Conferences have to include traditional 'union-bashing'. Sir John Methven referred on 6 November 1979 to the unions' 'wrong arguments' and to 'the damage they've done to our society and to themselves by grabbing more and more pay for less and less production'. Sir Anthony Bowlby, a retired industrialist, appealed on 12 April for the co-operation of the CBI and the TUC as 'social partners' for the benefit of the whole of British industry. He agreed privately later that this kind of co-operation is made more difficult by the speeches of CBI leaders which denounce 'union power'.

The unions would be much more ready for collaboration if they were treated more responsibly, as if they were capable of responsibility. There are, of course, irresponsible members of unions. However, the elected leaders of the unions usually are mature persons who will respond to friendliness and courtesy. It is with such men that management normally has to deal and will continue to have to deal. In fact many managers prefer to deal with the leaders of disciplined bodies, and some for that reason accept the closed shop (where all employees are union men) more readily than others. It is difficult, however, for management to accept strike calls 'from above', when, for example, engineers or steelworkers are called out from firms where they work contentedly, because their national unions have decided on a strike (often without a ballot). Yet it must be remembered (and it is indeed frequently said) that union power is passing to the shop floor. In so far as this is true, it gives to management an opportunity of achieving such a relationship with its workers as may even insulate the shop from national stoppages in certain circumstances. If there is any truth in the common allegation that national union officials have to justify themselves by resorting to national industrial action, local officials with rising shop floor power are capable of resisting if a mature trust relationship with management has been achieved. Such a relationship, however, can be achieved only by a dedicated management, one which keeps close in body and spirit to its workers.

It is sometimes alleged that national union leaders are anxious to retain central and personal power over the unions and their members by maintaining and employing the authority to call men out on industrial action. On the whole, recent history suggests that this is not the case. Union leaders are, for one reason or another, showing restraint. On the other hand, TUC leaders are asking to be taken into consultation about the future of industry and showing willingness to accept responsibility within industry. It is not beyond the bounds of possibility that union leaders, recognizing a shift in the balance of power within the unions, may become steadily more willing to accept new roles in co-operation with Government and management, in order to assist in the fuller involvement of labour in its work and in the cause of productivity. In an attempt to end at an early date the steel strike which began in January 1980, the four manual workers' unions made an offer to the British Steel Corporation 'proposing to set up joint multi-union bodies at national and local level to monitor productivity deals'.[2] Such an offer ought not necessarily to be treated with cynicism.

There are various signs of increasing TUC willingness to accept responsibility in industrial relations. These may not at first be successful (as in union attempts to limit secondary picketing). Yet they should not be sneered at, especially as they suggest a new role for national unions and one basically constructive. In a recent official report the TUC General Council pleads for co-operation in technological development 'by Government in conjunction with industry and trade unions'. It 'high-lights the need for initiatives by Government, employers and trade unions to meet the challenges posed by the advance in technology'.[3] These are expressions of a willingness, indeed of a burning zeal, to share responsibility, suggesting that just treatment of trade unionism might lead to just conduct by the unions.

Of course, there is intransigence, ignorance, stupidity. The Finniston *Report* speaks of 'antipathy to technology-based change and innovation . . . from company employees and their unions'. It goes on to say that 'there is clearly a need for a massive programme planned to educate and retrain employees of all ages and all levels if the human skills and support required to implement and sustain new technologies are to match demands for them'. A management that really knows how to communicate to its work force can help workers to see that the future of employment in this country depends upon the development of new technology and new industry, rather than upon a vain attempt at all costs to protect jobs in the old industries. 'It is growth in the number and diversity of new manufacturing enterprises to replace obsolete and declining industries which will provide extra jobs, and the need is to achieve this at least on the scale of those displaced in "traditional" industries', says the *Report*. It appeals: 'We hope that these considerations will lead the trade union movement to adopt an even more positive policy towards technology-based innovation in manufacturing and to encourage their members to support the introduction of innovations into industry and to participate in their operation.'[4]

Sir Anthony Bowlby was formerly a director of Guest, Keen and Nettlefold. He declared on 12 April 1980 that the countries which were losing most jobs owing to the development of technology were in fact the countries with least unemployment. But it was Lord Scanlon, one of the most prominent trade union leaders in Britain before his retirement, who gave his blessing emphatically to the new technology in his maiden speech in the House of Lords on 27 February 1980. Speaking on the Finniston *Report*, he said: 'I wish to declare . . . a very vital interest in the outcome of the Government's consideration of the Finniston *Report*.' He went on to quote from the *Report*: 'Industry must establish the rewards and prospects for good engineers which will attract more of the country's young people into a highly demanding engineering formation and thence into manufacturing industry.'[5] This kind of wisdom is to be found among trade unionists. Mr Terry Duffy, Hugh Scanlon's successor at the AUEW, on 1 April was seen on ITN declaring 'We want British Leyland to survive.' Here are men who speak English clearly, share understanding, are capable of growth. It is a shame if the practice of 'union-bashing' is to drive them into the unhelpful negativity of defence mechanisms.

The keen trade unionist is trying to grow into new spheres of constructive experience. The Jim Conway Foundation (of trade unionists), for example, is organizing week-end courses on 'Inflation and Economic Growth', 'Microtechnology and Industrial Change' and 'The Energy Crisis'. It has also arranged a series of day conferences for unionists on 'Aspects of Microtechnology' (and all this during a short period in 1980). It is this forward-looking, concerned, thoughtful type of trade union thinking of which the popular newspaper reader and television viewer remains ignorant. Given encouragement and helped towards a sense of responsibility, the trade unionist is capable of creativity in his thinking and his action. On the one hand, he needs encouragement. On the other, sensitivity must be shown towards his fear of redundancy.

One of the objects of this book is to assist those in no danger of redundancy and unemployment to realize just how sensitive this issue is. Trade unions as a whole share a sense that management often keeps them too long in the dark concerning pending danger of redundancy. Management's fear of giving unnecessary warning is understandable. Yet when the blow falls late in the day, the effect upon relationships may be very serious. When, in February 1980, BL Cars Division was obliged, owing to the fall in sales of its cars, to give 30,000 workers warning of a lay-off for a limited period in the near future, the consternation at Cowley was considerable. The chief union negotiator, Grenville Hawley, protested: 'The company would have been well advised to have discussed the matter with the trade unions before making the sensational announcement.'[6] It is difficult to disagree with Mr Hawley.

What the unions and the unionists are in one way or another, consciously or unconsciously, demanding is what is called justice. That means basically a fair deal for human beings and for all that relates to their identity. Management too has a right to expect justice from its workers. I shall develop a little later the meaning of the concept of justice. For the moment let me say that it implies respect: respect for human beings individually and respect also for associations of human beings. In a pluralist society such as ours we have a right to 'belong' and a right to ask for respect for what we belong to.

This book, and especially this chapter, is an attempt to promote the adoption and application of the principle of justice throughout industry. Justice is no meaningless word, and the practice of justice is something in which all believe and which most think capable of realization. A London taxi-driver knew exactly what was meant and what should be done about it, when I asked him what he thought of justice. 'There's not enough of it,' was his quick reply. He did not, in the course of conversation, seem to be a militant or a communist, but merely one who felt strongly that there was right and wrong about relationship in community. What was right for him was summed up in the word 'justice'.

The late Professor R. H. Tawney, of Balliol College, Oxford and of the London School of Economics, in his early days as a young Workers' Educational Association lecturer and Ratan Tata Foundation research student, noted in his *Commonplace Book* the problems of industry as he came to perceive and assess them. He wrote that divisions in society are caused by 'the consciousness of a moral wrong, and an outrage on what is sacred in man'. 'That is why,' he said, 'thousands of men strike in order that justice may be done to a few, when they have everything to lose, and nothing to gain by striking.' He went on: 'It is no use devising relief schemes for a community where the normal relationships are felt to be unjust.'[7] Tawney declared that peace would only come to industry 'when everyone recognizes that the material, objective, external arrangements of society are based on principles which they feel to correspond with their subjective ideas of justice'. 'The problem,' he wrote, 'is to find some principle of justice upon which human association for the production of wealth can be founded.' He quotes S. A. Barnett: 'Justice pays – if one is just enough.'[8] I sat under Professor Tawney at the London School of Economics. I remember vividly the excitement within myself when I suddenly began to see what he was driving at, when for a moment I began to share his vision of workers working like professional men, primarily for the joy of the job and only secondarily for the money to be earned for it. Tawney believed in that sort of professionalism. He wrote that 'the obligation of the maintenance of the service shall rest upon the professional organizations of those who perform it'.[9] He believed with all his heart in the capacity of trade unions and trade unionists to act responsibly. He would not have approved of those who write to the press or telephone to the BBC to deplore the 'wrecking tactics' of unionists in general. Such people are ignorant of the responsible determination of many unionists to maintain (and to develop, if possible) those industries on which their own jobs depend. They do not seriously seek to become redundant cast-offs of redundant companies.

Tawney, in writing of and pleading for justice, was expressing what the inarticulate feel. The London taxi-driver knew what justice meant and wanted more of it. Consciously or unconsciously, justice is on the minds of men. If cynics declare that for the working man 'justice' means self-interest, and the sophisticated argue that justice cannot be adequately distinguished from law, the man in the street knows perfectly well that justice is in fact different from self-interest and greater than law. At Plessey's of Liverpool, a senior shop steward returning from a prolonged shop stewards' meeting reacted to my mention of justice by saying that it was justice that the meeting was all about.

It is necessary not only to defend but to promote the use of the abstract term 'justice' in the discussion of industrial relationships. For the taxi-driver the word was clothed with meaning. For him the word signified important realities of which he felt men were deprived. In appealing for a hard look at the concept of justice in industrial relations, we are appealing on behalf of a high principle. We are in fact pleading that a new appeal and recourse to principle be made. Too long and too often have bargaining and negotiation taken place with little or no principle on either side. It has been all too often a power struggle, with scant reference to any aims other than increased wages and reduced hours. In this country, a nation dependent upon industry and in serious present straits, appeals for restraint, for productivity, for 'pulling together' are common. These appeals have little effect, but continue to be made. An appeal to the high principle of justice may be more helpful, for both sides of industry claim to accept that principle. R. H. Tawney wrote in 1921 that 'the industrial problem, in fact, is a matter of right'. That is what many men feel in their bones, and that is what makes some go madly into 'wildcat' action. Tawney wrote also that 'an appeal to principles is the condition of any reconstruction of society'.[10] It seems that nothing short of reconstruction is necessary for an industrially failing society. There must be a proclamation and a grasping of principles if there is to be this reconstruction.

An industrial correspondent in *The Times* calculates that the cost of the possible collapse of British Leyland, if that collapse were precipitated by industrial strife, would be the redundancy of 375,000 persons employed by BL or by those component manufacturers dependent upon it.[11] When such contingencies have to be considered seriously, we are in an area of potential national disaster. At such a time we need to ask ourselves whether it might not be right for both sides of industry to accept the moral principle of the doing of justice as the prime aim in industrial relationships. Concerning the importance of increased productivity, Tawney said that 'plenty depends upon co-operative effort, and co-operation upon moral principals'.[12] The present lack of productivity is certainly no advertisement for the present lack of moral principles in industrial relationships.

At the cost of repetition, let us be clear that we are pleading for the conscious taking into consideration in all industrial relations of the duty to aim at and work for the rendering of justice. It is true that to some the word will sound out of place; to others it will sound politically loaded. The word has recently been used so little that one might reasonably assume that it has been thought of very little too. In a world where much injustice has obviously been done (in Kampuchea, in Afghanistan, in Central America amongst other places) it would be tragic if we were to lose sight of and interest in it at home. The British have enjoyed a tradition of recognizing injustice, of calling it by its right name, of being outraged by the lack of it. The economist, F. A. Hayek, recalls the lament of a still older man, Albert Schweitzer: 'We are living at a time when justice has vanished. . . Our trust in justice has been utterly destroyed.'[13] These are terrible words; it may be that our minds need to be re-quickened over the fundamental importance of justice amongst human beings. The central thesis of this book is that what men primarily owe to one another is justice.

I propose in this chapter to reappraise the claim of certain Greek philosphers that 'justice' is the very basis of right relationship within community. In the next chapter we shall see how a comparable claim for justice is made in the Hebrew scriptures and how this Old Testament teaching is reinforced in that of the New Testament and of the Christian church.

Justice was the study of civilized men for over two millennia before social justice was ever spelled out by Karl Marx. The ancient Greek philosophers spoke not only to their own time, but loudly and clearly to ours, and Greek thought has left its mark wherever Graeco-Roman civilization has spread.

Bruno Snell declares that in fourth-century Greece 'something new was added' to Greek thought, 'and that was sympathy with one's fellow-man'. It was here and at this time, he says, that the concept of the dignity of man conquered the philosophical thought of Greece.[14] Of Plato and his writings it has been bravely said that 'the safest general characterisation of the European philosophical tradition is that it consists of a series of footnotes to Plato.'[15] No higher tribute was ever paid to any writer. Justice, for Plato, was the standard and rule of any society which valued unity. Speaking of justice as a quality vital for the state, he wrote that 'we must stand like hunters round a covert and make sure that justice does not escape us and disappear from view'.[16] Surely in the midst of modern altercations this warning challenges all in industry.

It could be pointed out that the Greek word for justice (dikaiosunē) meant not only justice but morality as a whole. It stood for morality as a personal quality and for morality as it issues in right attitude and action towards others. Desmond Lee speaks of the difficulty faced by the translator because of the wide overtones of the Greek word.[17] Nevertheless in some of his writings, Plato restricted the meaning of the word. He described the life of a society in which all were to play their individual roles, all thus to be fulfilled, all to fit together in harmony, each contributing his unique part to the whole. In this context, Plato defined justice as the principle that one man should do one job, the one for which he is most naturally suited.[18] This is by no means an unworthy aim, however difficult to realize. He says yet more strongly that if anyone in society is guilty of interfering with the role of another member of society, he is committing the worst of evils.[19] He considers the greatest wrong one can do to society is to commit an injustice.

For Aristotle, a generation after Plato, justice is basic altruism. Aristotle is quoting when he writes: 'Justice is the good of others'.[20] A group of modern monks echoes him when they say that justice is 'concerned with objective relations between men'.[21] Aristotle has in mind an underlying 'law of nature', an unwritten code of justice towards others, a 'custom of all or the majority of men', distinguishing (as he says) what is honourable from what is base.[22] Justice for Aristotle has become a positive attitude towards one's fellow-citizens. 'Justice . . . then, is complete virtue; virtue

. . . in relation to somebody else,' virtue exercised in relation to another person.[23]

From the fourth-century teaching of these great Greek philosophers has come a doctrine and a principle of Graeco-Roman civilization that belongs to the Europe which has inherited that civilization. It is the doctrine and the principle that every man in community, different though he be from every other, has his honourable part to play in that community. All in community owe respect to each individual, both because he is human and because he is a partner in community. This respect, due from man and due to man, we call justice.

John Rawls, the outstanding modern philosopher of justice, declares that it is from Aristotle that the more familiar formulations of social justice derive. 'Justice,' says Rawls, 'is the first virtue of social institutions.' He says that Aristotle means by justice a 'refraining . . . from gaining some advantage for oneself by seizing what belongs to another, his reward, his office, and the like, or by denying a person that which is due to him, the fulfillment of a promise, the repayment of a debt, the showing of proper respect and so on'. Rawls declares that 'laws and institutions no matter how efficient and well-arranged must be reformed or abolished if they are unjust'.[24] He sees society as an association of men joined together in co-operation and governed by a common acceptance of justice.

A philosophical case has been made for the paramount importance of justice in any society. The man without philosophy accepts this because he simply feels it to be true. The ordinary man has, in fact, a very real sense of justice and a clear grasp of what he means by the concept. As Sam Weller said, 'justice is a very different thing from the law'. Mr Bill Sirs, of the Iron and Steel Trades Confederation, is quite clear too about the distinction between law and justice. When the Appeal Court, headed by Lord Denning, ruled against his union in January 1980, Mr Sirs and the union accepted that 'the law was paramount'. He declared that his union was 'law-abiding', but he added that some of his members felt that 'a grave injustice had been done'.[25]

A society striving to raise the level of industrial relations by the promotion of justice in the industrial community is likely to find understanding and response from its members. Aristotle clearly stated that the 'legal is different from justice'.[26] The mid-nineteenth-century American, Henry Thoreau, remarked aptly that 'law never made a man a whit more just'.[27] The law appears to man to come upon him from outside. On the other hand, it is in the depth of the human mind that justice is enthroned. Society must take care that law reflects justice and does not clash with it. Lord Hailsham of Saint Marylebone, Lord Chancellor of England, writes to me that 'society must frame rules which have to be enforced, which means that they must be based on justice'. The justice is basic, and prior to the law.

Some do not care for the word 'justice'; some are nervous of it, and would prefer to use the word 'fairness'. John Rawls equates the two words, writing of 'justice as fairness'.[28] 'Fairness' is a more popular word with management. The Joint Managing Director of a group of firms making building and other products tells me that he prefers the concept of fairness 'because it has no legal connotation and because it has less of a confrontation sound about it'. Giles Ecclestone, General Secretary of the General Synod Board for Social Responsibility, writes to me that he commends the use of the word 'fairness'. 'It has rather different overtones,' he explains, 'and doesn't in particular entail implied judgments about the basic structures of industry.' It is sad that a strong philosophical (and biblical) word like 'justice' should have acquired implications which impede its employment and make some good men prefer to avoid it.

The suggestion being made here is that prejudice against the use of the word should be faced frankly and overcome. It is interesting to read the work of two sociologists, Richard Hyman and Ian Brough, who write of 'the confident and extensive use made in industrial relations of the idea of fairness'.[29] Yet, without intending to deprecate its use, they go on to say that to some extent 'it represents a secondary or derivative concept'. Questions of fairness, they explain, arise normally in the limited context of the distribution of benefits or duties among individuals or groups. Dr Kevin Hawkins again is helpful. 'Fairness,' he says, 'is based on comparison.'[30] In industrial relations, however, one needs to search for a principle which is self-authenticating, for foundations, for the primary and basic structures of relationships within industry or factory or plant. Such considerations surely require the concept of justice; the word 'fairness' is inadequate.

In industrial relations as a whole, nevertheless, use of the word 'fairness' has its place. Like 'justice', it has its political implications: it has long been associated in trade union parlance with the watch-word of 'a fair day's pay for a fair day's work'. In the period of established trade unionism, say Huw Beynon and Theo Nichols, fairness has come to mean the winning of a percentage on the given wage, the right of the union to be listened to, and the bringing up to standard of the worst employers.[31] The Tannoy Group in its *Statement of the Management Philosophy of Tannoy Ltd* proclaims 'the need to experience a sense of fairness in the way one is treated at work'. It goes on: 'By fairness, we mean that all employees should be justly rewarded according to the efforts and contribution they make to the company. . . We also consider that it is important to operate work standards which are felt to be fair and equitable for every job.' People believe that justice means more than all this. If we are to appeal for a new start in industrial relations, better to plead for justice. It can inspire.

It may be argued against the use of both words (and concepts) that there is often within industry no agreement as to what in fact is just (or fair). A Joint Shop Stewards' Committee at British Leyland, Cowley, complained in December 1977 in a 'Communiqué' that workers had to park their cars at a distance from their factory, while the staff were allowed to park their cars near their offices. It also claimed that there was resentment concerning the provision of separate lavatories and separate canteens for staff and workers. The staff, on the other hand, might have reasonably argued for the justice of all these arrangements, considering the size and shape of the Cowley complex and the nature of the work done by the staff. It is not impossible that, with contact and understanding, both parties might have come to agree about what was just. It might not perhaps have been quite so easy to resolve the same shop stewards' claim that executives were unjustly allowed to buy spare parts for their BL cars more cheaply than workers. However, with dialogue and a will for justice on both sides, it is conceivable that there too an arrangement seen by both parties to be just might have been reached. Baroness Wootton writes that 'it matters as much that justice should be manifest as that it should be done'.[32]

The disparity between managemental salaries and workers' pay might look like a much more serious problem to decide justly. The Chief Executive of British Leyland until November 1977, Mr Alex Park, received a salary of £47,000. This seems quite a large sum. However, Lord Grade, the TV and films tycoon, received a salary which dropped from £210,428 to £195,208 during the financial year 1978–79. He commented that he thought that the cutting of his salary to the lower figure was 'cheek'.[33] These larger figures are uncommon. The National *Analysis of Salaries and Wages*, published by Reward Regional Surveys and based on detailed information from 153 small and medium-sized companies, showed that in 1979 'financial controllers' received a 'medium salary' of £9000, sales managers £8166, works managers £7700. These are not figures of a kind to provoke gross resentment amongst workers, all well aware of what taxation does to income. The fact that some management jobs are rewarded with fringe benefits such as the use of a company car does not excite the average worker; nor does the fact that the top 10% income group receive 13.1% of their income from investment.[34] These are matters he scarcely thinks about. Mr Terry Duffy of the AUEW could not be persuaded in a radio interview of May 1980 to condemn a relatively large salary for the new Chairman of British Steel. Mr Henry Wilkins, of Wilkins and Mitchell of England, claims that his workers would be worried if he did not drive a Rolls-Royce. Simon Fraser, formerly of the Liverpool Trades Council, was emphatic to me that there is no resentment among workers concerning what management is paid. Managemental salaries out of all proportion to workers' wages are more likely to be the subject of obscene jokes than of burning indignation. In a society more thoughtful and more trained in the logic of justice, it is conceivable that large disparities of income might become unacceptable to many on both sides of industry. In the society of today, however, they are, broadly speaking, acceptable, and the two sides have not at present any serious difficulty concerning the justice (or injustice) of these disparities.

Far more serious and persistent and debatable a problem is that of differentials between the wages of skilled and unskilled labour. The skilled worker, the craftsman, claims a higher wage because of his skill, and because of his training for that skill. Two examples are provided by the Agricultural Wages Board pay award of 10 December 1979, and by British Leyland Cars' *Draft Agreement* of 7 November 1979 respectively, in both of which the differentials are thought by the skilled workers to be inadequate, and in the case of BL workers, by the unskilled to be too great. Farm workers are divided into four grades. A cowman belongs to Grade 1, because he is not only in charge of the cattle but has two full-time workers under him. The Agricultural Wages Board awards him £78.30. The tractor driver, also a skilled man, is awarded £66.70. These rates (from the Agricultural Wages Order 1980) compare with the unskilled labourer's award of £58.00. The farmer may not be at all keen on union activity amongst workers who are mostly not union men, yet he is inclined to believe that the differential won is not high enough. A Gloucestershire farmer points out to me that the cowman has many skills of the veterinary surgeon and that he is in charge of cattle that may be worth thousands of pounds. The tractor driver may be in charge of a vehicle worth £17,000. Of course, for many (but not for all) there are 'tied houses', free accommodation and often free solid fuel and milk. Farmers feel that agricultural workers are normally dedicated men, and that the skilled ones deserve high wages.

As for BL Cars, under the 'final draft' March 1980 proposals, there are five basic rates of pay in the pay structure for five different grades of worker. In Grade 5 there are the lift attendant, the toilet cleaner, the sweeper; in Grade 1 there are the bricklayer, the die toolmaker, the wood machinist (and others). The Grade 5 man is to be paid £73.50, plus a maximum bonus of £15.00; the Grade 1 man is to be paid £98.00, with a bonus of £15.00. *The Guardian* comments: 'BL has offered a 5 per cent rise to most of the workers, with 10 per cent for the 10,000 craftsmen. But the unions say that this upsets the differentials established in last year's wage parity agreement . . . and they are demanding the same percentage increase for all.'[35] By 'the unions', of course, is meant the unions under the influence of the great non-craftsmen's union, the TGWU.

Nothing seems more plain to the trained, skilled worker than his right to a considerably higher wage than that of the unskilled, untrained worker. It is difficult for a professional man, and far from easy for a production worker, to realize the strength of feeling amongst skilled workers. This is not merely a feeling in favour of a high differential, but a belief that skilled workers need to negotiate on their own because only they can understand their own skills and needs. It is this claim for separate negotiations for skilled workers which lies behind Mr Roy Fraser's unofficial United Craft Organization. Roy Fraser is an AUEW convener in BL who has been leading his fellow toolmakers (and other craftsmen) in a demand since 1976 for 'the right of the skilled to sell their own skills'. The company has shown some understanding and sympathy for his argument; but the union, with its large majority of unskilled members and its officers elected by that majority, has withheld support. Because of that lack of support for the due recognition of the claims of skilled labour, Mr Fraser's United Craft Organization remains unofficial, unrecognized by the AUEW. The AUEW cannot support these skilled men's claims, because it is competing for the support of unskilled workers with the TGWU. Here is trade unionism at its worst. In this unhappy sphere of inter-union rivalry we are in a situation where justice seems to be sacrificed to numbers. This is power politics, and the unions need to look hard at the justice (or the injustice) of it all.

The wage demanded by the United Craft Organization for skilled workers in BL in 1979 was scarcely different from the wage offered to skilled workers under the company's parity scheme, provided that they reach their production targets, but it assumed a larger differential. The skilled worker in BL believes that he is entitled to a bigger recognition of his skill and of his training for that skill. We are up against the pride of the skilled worker and the jealousy of the unskilled worker; we are also up against inter-union competition.

Above and beyond all this, we must face up to the failure of British industry to secure the skilled labour it requires. Mr Fraser claims, and much of British industry would agree, that it is the present shortage of skilled labour which obliges British manufacturers to import many of the products of skilled labour from overseas. A survey by the Manpower Services Commission and the National Economic Development Office covered 110 companies in an area around Reading in 1979. It found there were shortages of several kinds of skilled manual worker and of qualified engineers and technicians. For many trades, including fitters, machine tool setters, tool makers and welders, a majority of vacancies had been unfilled for three months. In a newly-equipped, highly up-to-date factory in Ebbw Vale, I looked almost in vain amongst the complicated and expensive machinery for any products of British engineering. In the end, I found one small machine.

In the British engineering industry, the number of skilled workers declined from 754,000 in 1965 to 566,000 in 1975. It is still declining. The Finniston *Report* refers to a 'national shortage of technicians' and to the 'diminution of pay differentials between workers and technicians in recent years, which have eroded the incentive to seek extra training and promotion from the shop floor'.[36] Skilled labour is vital for Britain if it is not to turn to Germany, Japan, the USA and France for the products of toolmakers and other craftsmen. A union report states that 'more and more tools are being imported from the USA or from Germany.

. . . Leyland's needs in these directions inevitably push it to Europe and the USA, where it takes its place at the end of the queue behind the regular customers of these companies.'[37] Above all, a supply of skilled workers is needed if the 'industrial robots', the computer-controlled automated machines of tomorrow's tool industry are to be made in Britain. There will be fewer workers and they will need longer training (perhaps as long as seven years).

It is clear that technological engineers are going to require proportionately higher differentials and there will be difficulties with the unions about these. A Midlands firm writes of problems 'in the recruitment and retention of engineers in the dynamics department', and of the need to make higher payments to these men 'with a new structure, new job titles in such a way as to minimize the risk of cross-reference by the unions to other departments'. A project engineer reports in frustration and dismay that he loses the services of highly qualified engineers, some with high degrees, whom he needs for computer development. He loses them because company agreements with the unions limit the pay he can offer these men. The needed differential cannot be offered. The jealousy of the less well-qualified wins the day and all are losers. The anti-differential spirit expressed by company agreements with the unions discourages the due rewarding of skill, training and experience. The company is damaged as the men move elsewhere. One who had moved wrote back to say that the system 'promoted the interest of the mediocre at the expense of the creative'. He wanted no further part in a company where the mediocre always came off best. Creativity is needed, and justice demands that it be rewarded. In one nationalized industry an engineer reported that after a great deal of hard work on a nuclear reactor he was not only personally thanked by management but also sent a £50 cheque. His delight was out of all proportion; tribute had been paid to skill and effort, and justice was seen to be at work. It all cost so little.

This Midlands firm writhes in its struggle to attract adequately qualified engineers, while continuing to offer them inadequate differentials. It fears the reactions of its workers and its unions if it offers the men it needs enough to attract them. Engineers want to be judged on merit; the best of them refuse to accept a pay structure which assumes that they fit into a certain category. That, they claim, is not so. It seems that the firm concerned does not feel able to run the risk of talking the whole problem over boldly and frankly with the men and unions most concerned. If there were a commitment by both sides to the doing of the just, a commonly accepted view of what is in the circumstances just might be worked out together. The vital need of the firm concerned for adequately qualified engineers might be jointly recognized and the price duly paid.

Craftsmen, we know, have left industry because of inadequate differentials. While Roy Fraser denies that his craftsmen are primarily concerned with differentials, the National Economic Development Office declared in 1977 that 'recent trends in wages, especially the erosion of differentials, make the retention of skilled labour more difficult'. It noted that the earnings of skilled engineering workers relative to labourers reached a peak in 1967. Since then there has been 'a steady and significant decline in the ratios, i.e. the percentage differential between skilled workers and labourers'. It said that the skilled workers' differential was near its lowest point in the last sixty years. This decline in differentials, it said, is common to all regions. It took the view that the trend has gone too far, and that it 'may be discouraging craftsmen from staying within the industry, possibly acting as a disincentive to potential entrants and providing little attraction for former engineering employees who may be considering returning to the industry'.[38]

BL toolmakers at Cowley earning £76 a week in 1979 claimed to me that wages up to £124 a week were being paid to toolmakers elsewhere in the United Kingdom. I myself saw an advertisement in a British newspaper for toolmakers who could earn £130 for a five-day week. It is well known that some very high wages for skilled workers are being paid in Germany. Dr Hawkins says: 'Differentials have a *market* function. They can either induce workers to enter a particular industry or occupation or discourage them from doing so.'[39] The skilled worker has no doubt of the justice of his case; the unskilled (or semi-skilled) scarcely thinks in terms of justice. It might be that, as men are encouraged to think more seriously about justice, the case for a considerable differential would become apparent even to those who do not qualify for one.

In the 1979 dispute concerning toolmakers and other skilled workers in BL, Sir Michael Edwardes, Chief Executive, went on television and radio to call Mr Fraser 'a wrecker'. Mr Fraser told me that he looked on this as 'part of the game' (in which one party attempts to stir public opinion against the other). Yet Mr Fraser is not an International Socialist, nor does he belong to the

Socialist Workers Party, nor does he have any anarchist sympathies. He rears his family and works on his allotment. Those who know him know him to be in no sense a wrecker. The charge could not be taken seriously. The Australian Gavin Sinclair writes wisely: 'Success can come to the militants only to the extent that employers play into their hands, which they do most of the time by concentrating their attention on the activities of the militants and by ignoring the genuine content of the original grievances.'[40] Very often, by violently attacking the militants, employers give them credibility as opponents and weld together moderate men with genuine grievances and the attacked militants. The more passion employers and politicians inject into their attacks on unions and unionists, the more they antagonize moderate men whom they could placate. These men, after all, know the militants and can judge them more fairly than employers can. With more agreement about the need to seek justice, emotionalism could play a less harmful role in industrial relations.

Roy Fraser claims quietly to me that he is concerned with justice rather than personalities. Sir Michael Edwardes would no doubt claim to be no less concerned for justice. The case for large differentials is open to debate. It ought to be debated by men who know and tolerate one another and are seeking for justice. There may even be an acceptable case in at least a minority of industries for parity of wages. This parity was achieved, with the agreement of all the unions and of most of the workers, both at the Govan Shipyard and at Chloride Batteries of Clifton Junction, Swinton. In both places, there were strong conveners. 'Yes,' Jimmie Airlie, formerly the Govan convener, wrote to me, 'there is pay parity at Govan.' There were also nearly 4000 men working there on the Govan share of a £115 million Polish order. Parity seemed to work. It seemed to work too at Chloride Batteries in 1978, but as we shall see when we look more closely at this company in chapter 8, parity has proved difficult to maintain.

In November 1977 a boilermaker in a shipyard, fighting for his traditional differential, was quoted as saying: 'They can have parity if they want it, but we shall have another increase.'[41] By nearly 2000 votes the 'outfitters' at Swan Hunter shipyard voted in accordance with this defiance. Yet the defiance did not last; there were Polish ships to build. A settlement was reached and the high differential was lost. What may at first seem to one side to be unjust may come to seem equitable if and when reasonable men sit down together in a reasonable frame of mind. Exactly how this process of sitting down together takes place over a considerable period of time in a Queensland mining company is explained in chapter 10. At some British shipyards, after the successful negotiation of the Polish order in 1978, Mr Ronnie Ferns, a welders' shop steward and a shipyard worker of thirty years' standing, reported co-operation among unions and between unions and management such as British shipyards had never seen before. Mr Ferns declared: 'The men leaned over backwards to meet the target date. They did things that they had never done before. They relaxed working practices; engineers, plumbers, building workers crossed demarcation lines to get the job done. . . We allowed sub-contractors to come in. We knew how important the Polish order was and that if we could meet the target dates we could prove we were viable. We skinned this industry down to its bare essentials.'[42] Despite the 'infection' of wage settlements here by wage settlements there, good on-the-spot relationships locally can be shown again and again to make possible wages and conditions different from place to place. A developed community spirit in a factory may and does frequently allow that factory to pay less; it is usually understood that it will pay more when it can. The problem of differentials has to be worked out amongst workers and unions. Understanding, tolerance, even generosity of mind may grow with wise leadership, with education and training, with the fellowship that justice breeds.

All too often, outraged men with different conceptions of what is just, or simply with a sense of opportunism and present power, come together only to quarrel and disperse. Mr G. A. Peers, from his wide experience of bargaining, emphasized to me over and over again the importance of frequent consultation outside times of crisis. In times of crisis, he said, power tends to win. Outside times of crisis, there is a chance for reason, a hope of agreement concerning what in the circumstances is just.

7 The Christian Doctrine of Justice

I believe that the serious adoption in industry of the principle and practice of justice would cause an improvement in relationships. I propose now to consider whether this has Christian as well as philosophical authority. Everyone who knows anything about Christianity knows something of its teaching of love. Very few seem to know anything of its teaching of justice. It has this teaching, yet at present it seems to have little to say that is of value for the improvement of industrial relations. This is a pity. There are within industry employers, managers, trade unionists prepared to listen to Christianity with respect when it talks sense.

There are many who believe that Christianity can have nothing practical to say of value in a technical and complicated area such as industrial relations. This is perhaps a measure of the failure of the church. If the church of Christ is to represent the person whose name it bears, if it is to stand amongst men for the God who is present with people and for his kingdom which is 'upon' us, it must be concerned with all that concerns its members and God's people. As R. H. Tawney rightly said: 'In every city, however unholy, there is God.'[1] No serious Christian who believes in the transcendence of God fails also to believe in his immanence 'in us'[2] (or better, as the Greek permits, 'with us'). Any idea that this God has nothing to do with man's economic problems, or that the Christian must not bring his religion to bear on every kind of relationship, is quite contrary to Christianity.

'To worship God without a social conscience is idolatrous,' said Bishop Michael Ramsey, former Archbishop of Canterbury, speaking on 31 January 1980 about the great Oxford social theologian and preacher, Henry Scott Holland. The church is concerned with its God and his Christ as it seeks them, finds them, represents them in modern society, within industry itself. It may choose to remain silent or, in its foolishness, it may choose to talk nonsense. Of its right to speak on behalf of God on what concerns him there is no doubt. Professor David Jenkins of the William Temple Foundation says that we are required 'to make determined and disciplined efforts to draw on our Christian experience and traditions in relation to present personal, social and political pressures'.[3] He goes on: 'We know God is in reality and the fulfiller of reality . . . we have to choose entry-points in our surroundings for working at particular human problems where faith can be both exercised and learnt.' 'The God known in and through Jesus,' he writes, 'is also known in and through the contemporary.'[4] This he declares to be typical of prophetic religion. He is saying that the God whom the prophets of Israel encountered in their days is the God whom we encounter in and through our days. The Christian must indeed seek entry-points into experience of God in his own environment, in industry if he works there. Let him seek God there; let him seek knowledge of God's will there. If he seeks he will find. The ordinary Christian quietly, rather than bishops loudly, may be called to be the voice of the church there. Where relations are bad, someone must speak for God to his people in a language which they can understand.

Let no one imagine that what is required of the Christian prophet in or for the factory is the preaching of love. Love is not the attribute of the neophyte but the quality of the proficient. Christians who have often themselves failed in the practice of love can scarcely preach it to men and women of all faiths and none in industry. Mother Basilea, of the German Sisterhood of Mary, writes that after twenty years of hard work in community work greatly blessed, she is still 'struggling to be loving', 'a long way off from perfect love'.[5] Reinhold Niebuhr declares that experience proves that the real problem of existence is that we ought to love one another and do not.[6] In view of all this, Christians must be careful what they say to others about love.

Let there be no fantasies about love in industrial life. A correspondent in the *Oxford Diocesan Magazine* writes of the 'Christian' Middle Ages: 'The baker sold . . . with love. Love for his friends; love for the loaf . . . love for the materials he had used.'[7] This, of course, is not history. Love did not come easily to Christians in the Middle Ages any more than it comes easily today. If love is the Christian goal, it is certainly not the way along which Christians (and others) find it easy to travel. Even for the devout, love is not easy. Yet there is a stepping-stone towards love; and that is the acceptance and practice of justice. In the Encyclical *Anno Quadragesimo*, Pope Pius XI clearly taught that charity cannot take the place of justice. Justice must come first; upon its foundation love can be built up. The Christian believes that the teaching and doing of justice is a necessary prerequisite for the teaching and doing of love.

Outstanding Christian witnesses testify to this truth. The distinguished Protestant theologian, Emil Brunner, declared that 'justice is always the pre-condition of love'. He went on: 'The real gift of love begins where justice has been done.' He wrote of 'the divine law of justice', claiming that 'love . . . always presupposes justice and fulfils the claims of justice before setting about its own business'.[8] Reinhold Niebuhr wrote magisterially that justice which demands equality of treatment makes an approximation to love.[9] It is a basis and a beginning.

The Christian mind of today appears often to be so concentrated upon the law of love (which the Christian apologizes for not fulfilling) that the point needs to be laboured that the law of justice as his prime duty to man (and which he can fulfil) tends to be ignored by the Christian. John Bennett, the former President of Union Theological Seminary, tries to show how one law in fact implies the other. 'Love should will justice. . . ,' he writes. 'Love and justice come together.'[10] Some modern Benedictines put it well: 'If charity is to be efficacious it must first be concerned for justice. Justice is concerned with the objective relationships between men.' Of justice itself they declare that 'the search for justice is a basic Christian duty'.[11]

The significant primacy which is claimed for justice in both Catholic and Protestant thought requires evidence from the Bible where the foundations for the claim are to be found. There indeed the foundations are, in the Old Testament, amongst the roots of the Christian religion. The Hebrew teaching of justice begins with the justice of God. 'The Lord is just and loves just dealing' (Ps. 11.7). 'The Lord is a lover of justice' (Ps. 37.28). 'God's throne is built upon righteousness and justice' (Ps. 89.14). There is nothing mealy-mouthed about the strong Old Testament assertions of the essential justness of God. 'The Lord is a God of justice' (Isa.30.18). Isaiah is clear concerning God as the divine source of justice: 'I have bestowed my spirit upon him, and he will make justice shine on the nations . . . he will make justice shine on every race . . . he will plant justice on earth (Isa. 42.1–4). When the young Edward Bouverie Pusey claimed that scripture nowhere says that God is justice, he was scarcely being fair to scripture.

The Old Testament describes a 'covenant' relationship in which, in most references, the people are assumed to be under obligations to God who has promised them his protection. Dr John Bright describes early Israel as a 'sacral league . . . formed in covenant with Yahweh and under the rule of Yahweh'.[12] Dr J. H. Cone goes further: 'The covenant not only places upon Israel the responsibility of accepting the absolute sovereignty of Yahweh as defined in the first commandment; it also requires Israel to treat the weak in her midst as Yahweh has treated her.'[13] Commentators disagree as to the period in which the covenant concept originated. Recent scholarship indicates that it only reached its classical form in the relatively late time of the book of Deuteronomy.[14] Nevertheless, the obligation of justice towards the weak, together with the so-called 'laws of humaneness and righteousness', are proclaimed loudly in Exodus 20, 22 to 23, 19, the 'Book of the Covenant'. These moral obligations long predate Deuteronomy. In the Book of the Covenant there is to be found an exaltation of justice. The Israelites were told in no uncertain language not to join the majority of men in the practice of injustice, not to rob the poor of the justice that is due to them. 'Nor . . . shall you side with the majority to pervert justice. . . You shall not deprive the poor man of justice (Ex. 23.3,6). In these passages from the 'Book of the Covenant', the word for justice (*mishpat* in Hebrew) concerns specifically the justice of the Israelite law-courts, of 'the elders in the gate' (where justice was administered in early Hebrew settlements). The word, however, does not refer merely to a man-made legal code and administration. *Mishpat* was always in Hebrew thought connected with the divine; it was God's justice that was being administered in the gate. 'Justice,' says N. H. Snaith, was 'closely intertwined with religion'.[15] The word *tsędeq* (normally translated 'righteousness') implies an attitude creative of fellowship between two parties. *Mishpat* means *tsędeq* in practice, the doing of righteousness. Thus the prophet Amos calls justice 'the fruit of righteousness' (Amos 6.12, RSV).

Man is called to be just because God is~~just; God's~~ justice requires man's justice. The Hebrews, the people of a just God, people in a covenant-relationship with him, a communion-alliance, came to understand that this just God demanded a just people. 'To do what is right and just' is 'to conform to the way of the Lord,' says God, concerning Abraham, the father-founder of the Hebrew race. 'Endow the king with thy own justice,' sings the psalmist. (Ps. 72.1). Indeed, as H. H. Rowley has written, justice stood for true religion.[16] For the Hebrews, Eichrodt declared, justice was no abstract thing, but denoted the rights and duties of parties in fellowship.[17]

Hundreds of years, therefore, before the great Greek philosophers, the Hebrew people worshipping Yahweh were growing into a respect for justice no less than that of Plato and Aristotle. Indeed some modern commentators on the Psalms believe that the majority of them belong, at least basically, to the pre-exilic days of the kings of Judah and Israel.[18] Yehezkel Kaufmann, writing in Hebrew at the Hebrew University in Jerusalem, says that psalm literature in general was stereotyped in pre-exilic times. 'The collections that eventually comprised the book of Psalms are all pre-exilic.'[19] This brings us back to the seventh century before Christ (or earlier). 'Cloud and mist enfold him, righteousness and justice are the foundation of his throne' (Ps. 97.2); 'Justice looks down from heaven . . . Justice shall go in front of him and the path before his feet shall be peace' (Ps. 85, 11,13). The people of Israel may indeed have sung of God's justice, before the eight-century prophets preached it. I am emphasizing the Old Testament teaching of justice and its antiquity to show how the conception of a just God calling his people to justice is embedded deeply in the religion out of which Christianity sprang.

As for the eighth-century prophets, those Christians who have not listened carefully to their demands for justice and their denunciations of the lack of it have not heard the Word of God. The great Isaiah of Jerusalem (and of the king's court) declared that God 'looked for justice and found it denied, for righteousness but heard cries of distress' (Isa. 5.7). The earliest of the eighth-century prophets, Amos, the herdsman of Tekoa, proclaimed God's dramatic demand on his people, that Israel should dispense with religious triviality, so that God's justice might come down upon the nation. 'Spare me the sound of your songs,' he cries in God's name. 'I cannot endure the music of your lutes. Let justice roll on like a river, and righteousness like an ever-flowing stream' (Amos 5.23,24). Not the music of Israelite worship, but justice and righteousness are required, justice and righteousness pouring down like floods after the winter rains, persisting like the wadis that do not run dry in the summer drought.

The great Isaiah, a little later, pictured a king descended from David who would rule his kingdom 'with justice and righteousness' who would 'judge the poor with justice and defend the humble in the land with equity (Isa. 9.7; 11.4). The prophet Micah challenged contemporary kings and their advisers. 'Listen,' he said, 'leaders of Jacob, rulers of Israel, you . . . make justice hateful and wrest it from its straight course (Micah 3.9). If all these words concerning kings and rulers seem a little remote from the managers and shop stewards whom we have been looking at, a message is coming over from Micah which makes sense to modern ears: 'God has told you what is good: and what is it that the Lord asks of you? Only to act justly, to love loyalty, to walk wisely before your God (Micah 6.8). To 'act justly', meant not merely to keep the law, but to uphold God's will in conduct.

Professor Bernhard Anderson, of Princeton Theological Seminary, sums up this eighth-century prophetic doctrine of justice: It is 'the fulfillment of responsibilities that arise out of particular relationships within the community. . . Each relationship has its specific obligation and all relationships are bound ultimately to God. . . When the demands of various relationships are fulfilled, justice . . . prevails and there is *salom*, peace.'[20] Out of this brief study of the Old Testament's teaching of justice comes clearly a Christian conception of justice as a positive, outgoing virtue, binding together in community those who practise it.

We turn now to the New Testament, not to a new religion but to a development of the old. Jesus said that he had not come to abolish the law and the prophets but to 'complete' them (Matt. 5.17). It needs to be said and seen that the New Testament teaches justice as clearly as the Old. Jesus proclaims quite clearly the 'old' commandment of justice. 'Always treat others as you would like them to treat you,' he says. 'That is the Law and the prophets' (Matt. 7.12). Here is plain teaching of justice: man should treat man with respect, man should respect others and treat them justly. This simple New Testament message rings bells in the minds of ordinary people. The man in the office, the man at the bench, is prepared to listen to that. When Jesus in this way speaks of the obligation to be just, he speaks a language that can be understood, a challenge which many can accept.

Let there be no mistake. The basic message of Jesus's gospel is not one of mere altruism, not even one of justice. The justice he taught was an element in a much greater concept, that of the kingdom of God. It is this doctrine of the kingdom which is fundamental; it is this which, above all, has to be taken seriously, at least by Christians. There is no mistaking that clear challenge at the beginning of St Mark's Gospel: 'Jesus came into Galilee proclaiming the Gospel of God: "The time has come; the kingdom of God is upon you" ' (Mark 1.14f.). The gospel is of the kingdom; the king is God; and as king he is to be obeyed and served. This is where the New Testament starts. 'The reign of God,' writes J. Bonsirven, the French Jesuit scholar, 'is . . . the centre, and may we say it, the whole of the specific message of Jesus and of his activity'.[21] He declares that the kingdom of God means not only the reign of God but the reign of a just God, under whom justice is pursued, justice is done. God's kingdom means that God's justice is honoured, his will for justice amongst us respected. When Christians begin to understand the meaning of the kingdom of God, we become at one with that religion in which the psalmist sang 'The Lord is king, let the earth be glad' (Ps. 97.1). St Paul understood what the kingdom meant. He wrote that 'the kingdom of God is not eating and drinking, but justice, peace, and joy' (Rom. 14.17). The late Professor Norman Perrin explained that the kingdom involved both the activity of God and the response of his people.[22] The author of the Epistle to the Ephesians declared that where the light of Christ is, there goodness, justice, truth spring up (Eph. 5.10). In God's kingdom, these things happen.

For Jesus and his church then the gospel is of the kingdom; the kingdom implies justice. Justice is fundamental to the kingdom; the kingdom is no kingdom of God without justice. Christians continue to sing the old Israelite song: 'So shall I talk of thy justice and of thy praise all the day long' (Ps. 35.28). Terrible and withering is Jesus's condemnation, according to the gospel accounts, of those 'lawyers and Pharisees' who, he says, 'pay tithes of mint and rue and every garden-herb, but have no care for justice' (Luke 11.42). They have overlooked, he says, the weightier demands of the Law, justice, mercy and good faith (Matt. 23.23). Such were the Pharisees and the experts in Jewish law of Jesus's time at their worst.

J. A. Baird goes so far as to say that 'there can be no doubt that for Jesus the controlling fact about the nature of God is his justice'. He declares that Jesus commands 'his disciples to be true to the Spirit within them, to the driving imperative of the God of

Justice whose presence always disturbs men with the thrust of a command'.[23] The reign of God begins with the establishment of justice. Later come the supreme laws of the kingdom: love of God and love of neighbour. Very gently, very firmly, Père Bonsirven writes that justice 'remains the preliminary condition for love'. 'Its violation', he says, 'causes . . . a wounding of love.'[24] Nor is the seeming conflict between the priority of justice and the primacy of love a new problem for a church nourished on the scriptures. There has been no lack of hard thinking concerning the role of justice in Christian (and other) life between New Testament times and those of Reinhold Niebuhr and Emil Brunner. Let us look briefly at the medieval Christian philosopher who tried to 'christianize' Aristotle. Aquinas had to rely on imperfect Latin translations from the Greek. Yet he grasped enough of the thought of Aristotle to ensure that the Greek doctrine of justice associated with the fourth-century philosophers, together with that of the eighth-century Hebrew prophets, should remain firmly incorporated in the Christian religion. St Thomas Aquinas is little read today; his style, his language, his reasoning make little appeal to the majority. Yet what he writes concerning justice certainly merits serious Christian consideration. He wrote of 'a special virtue, and this is justice'.[25] 'Justice,' he said 'directs man in his relations with other men.'[26] He declared that 'justice is a habit whereby a man renders to each man his due.'[27] He called it 'the perpetual and constant will to render to each one his right'.[28] He was quoting Aristotle when he wrote that 'the most excellent of the virtues would seem to be justice, and more glorious than the morning or the evening star.'[29] 'It is the master-virtue,' he said, 'commanding and prescribing what is right',[30] directing the good citizen to the common good.[31]

Few indeed study the scholastic philosophy of the mighty Aquinas today, yet those who do study it are profoundly influenced towards the just society. In the Middle Ages Aquinas made his point; he caused justice to be recognized as the basic social virtue. Dr A. J. Carlyle was able to write of medieval Christians that 'whatever their shortcomings, they did at least believe firmly that the first and last principle of social life was justice.'[32] Modern Christians may choose to despise medievalism and dismiss St Thomas Aquinas with the rest of the Middle Ages. But let them not despise or reject that great and ancient doctrine, that philosophical and biblical truth, that cardinal virtue of which psalmists sang, prophets preached and philosophers wrote, that justice to which

Christian kings were forced, at least at times, to subordinate their authority. The people of the Middle Ages, wrote Dr Carlyle, were clear that there was no legitimate authority which was not just, and which did not make for justice.[33] This was a not unworthy ideal. To recommend it at a time when ideals are needed to give inspiration in politics and industry is not to recommend a return to medievalism, but rather the right use of our Graeco-Christian heritage.

This chapter has been a plea to Christian people to take justice into their concept of the Christian religion. It has been a plea also to the non-Christian to take seriously the demand of the Bible for justice in social relationships. There is also implicit an appeal for leadership within the church, for leadership in the name of God, in the cause of social justice and for the healing of relationships in industry. There has been such leadership in comparatively recent times, but it came to an end tragically in 1944 with the death of Archbishop William Temple. In a foreword to the 1976 reissue of Temple's 1942 *Christianity and Social Order*, Edward Heath wrote that it 'brings home to every one of us the continuing importance of being able to rely on a body of principle by which our plans and our actions can be both motivated and judged'.[34] All who seek improvement in industrial relations, and all who are depressed by present lack of progress, would do well to take seriously that biblical and scholastic tradition to which Temple in his great wisdom appealed, that 'body of principle' which he had mastered and made his own. Of justice, the Archbishop wrote: 'The Christian cannot ignore a challenge in the name of justice. He must either refuse it or, accepting it, devote himself to removal of the stigma.'[35] Some who did not know him have held Temple to be naïve in his social thought. Edward Norman described that thought as 'second-hand' and 'inept'.[36] Those who knew or heard him, those who knew how he read, thought, reasoned, engaged in dialogue, would scarcely agree. His seeking, ever-growing learning was available in the 1939 war years to chaplains, officers, soldiers in Northern Command. 'Second-hand' is the last phrase which those of us who knew and worked with him would apply to him. I heard the news of his death from a Signals sergeant in the Burma jungle in 1944. The man spoke as if he had suffered a grievous personal loss, as if for him a light had gone out with Temple's dying. Bishop F. R. Barry, in almost his last writing in 1976 before his death, paid tribute to Temple as a prophet who stirred men's minds and wills.[37] He said that when people read

Temple's *Christianity and Social Order*, 'their pulses quickened and their hearts leaped up'. 'The charge against our system,' Temple had said, 'is one of injustice.'[38]

There must be many outside and inside industry who see no substance in that charge. Yet wherever there has been a refusal to listen, an unwillingness to think, an unwise action or a stupid failure to act, in so far as some have seen this to be unjust, there is need for investigation, for self-appraisement, for the possible seeking of another way. Industrial relationships will not right themselves when injustice seems to have been done. 'The enemy of justice,' said the good Benedictines, 'is often not so much malice or lack of goodwill, as blindness and lack of vision.'[39] In unsatisfactory times, Christians and men of good will ought to try to work together, to strive side by side for the vision of the community that should be, to face up penitently to faults perhaps in the past unrealized, to minister in practical ways to their fellow workers' good, to seek to see and to agree about what is just, and at all costs to do it. That way lies good relationship, common involvement in enterprise, peace in industry.

8 Participation

We have seen that in some areas at least British industrial productivity is unsatisfactory and that inadequate industrial relations are at least partially to blame. We have seen that these industrial relations are sometimes lacking in human quality, in that respect for fellow humans which was rightly described by the Greek philosophers and in the Bible as 'justice'. This justice thoughtful Christians recognize to be the sound basis for that higher virtue which we call love. Amongst many industrialists and amongst responsible trade unionists there is a will towards justice, an implicit respect for it, however little lip-service may be rendered to the word itself. We move on to consider how the principle of justice, of treating men with the respect due to them, is in fact being incorporated into industry and could be further incorporated.

Let us first of all consider what is called 'participation' (or 'workers' participation') to which respect is paid in employers' and trade union theory and in neutral publications such as the Industrial Society's *Participation – The Proven Code*.[1] When a church newspaper heads a news item on its front page 'Worker Participation in Industry?'[2], the question mark suggests ignorance concerning the worker participation which already exists. The question ought to be: 'Should there be more worker participation?' As long ago as 1917 the first Whitley Report affirmed the positive need for workers to have a greater opportunity for participation in and even some share in the control of parts of industry which particularly affect them.[3] It is, in fact, commonly agreed that workers must participate in some measure in decision-making in industry, even if this only means that they have a chance to air their views. Participation has been defined as 'the upward exercise of control by subordinates over various forms of organizational activity, with that control being exercised directly by the worker himself, or indirectly through some means of representation'.[4] Perhaps, to make allowance for different forms and degrees of participation to meet varying needs, the definition might be amended, for the present at least, to read 'the upward exercise of influence'. We shall study later the case for a real share by 'subordinates' in managemental control itself.

There is no doubt that when some unionists declare their belief in the right of management to manage, they mean that they emphatically do not want the responsibility of a share in management. Messrs Goodman and Whittingham quote a shop steward who said: 'I neither have the knowledge nor the desire to make policy for this company, and I have constantly to remind management that it is their job to manage.'[5] The CBI deliberately chose the phrase 'employee involvement' for its *Guidelines for Action for Employee Involvement* issued after the debate concerning participation during its 1978 conference. The word 'involvement' was chosen, it says, 'to avoid the emotional and political overtones of other words'. It continues: 'We are talking about the communication and consultation arrangements which are integral parts of 'an "open" style of management operated by managers with the necessary professional skills, self-confidence and pride in their job.' One is obliged to ask how 'open' is the style of management to be? What does the CBI really believe, really advocate? No doubt different members would give different answers. The *Guidelines* came after the expression of varying views at the 1978 conference. During this debate one speaker, cheered by others, was emphatic in declaring: 'Participation has become the most monumentally boring word in the English language, meaningless to the shop floor. What they are waiting for and yearning for is not the cosmetic device of participation, but the exercise of management authority, leadership.'

It may be that this sort of reaction is to the demand for participation of a kind for which the workers are not ready or for participation according to a pattern (perhaps imported from overseas). Rule 1 of the AUEW contains the statement that the first object of the union is 'the control of industry in the interests of the community'. The union scarcely appears to claim seriously that 'control' which the statement seems to demand. Mr Len Murray, of the TUC, speaking to his fellow unionists at the TUC Annual Congress of 1975, is more realistic when he says: 'We are tired of lectures, we are tired of appeals; we want to get involved, we want to work it out together.' That is quite different from 'controlling' industry. There is a sincerity and a rationality about this plea which one hopes that the CBI's *Guidelines* is responding to. CBI members (and others) would do well to worry and talk less about the 'power' which the unions are supposed to be trying to exert and to consider more seriously the unions' expressions of willingness to co-operate.

It is quite certain that there remains little enthusiasm among trade unionists for the 'taking over' of industry. About all this Dr Kevin Hawkins writes to me most sensibly: 'There are vast areas of company activity which are of little interest to shop stewards.' Yet he also writes that there is a 'demand by workers for more influence over decisions affecting their own jobs and working conditions, including the organization of work, the fixing of work standards and methods of payment'. Dr John Adair writes from a management background. He is Professorial Fellow in Leadership studies at the University of Surrey. He was formerly Adviser to Leadership Training at the Royal Military College, Sandhurst (1961–65). Addressing management with understanding of management, he declares: 'People desire more and more to participate in those decisions which affect their welfare at work.'[6]

Let us turn to the men actually in industry, to a prominent senior shop steward, Derrick George, of Chloride Limited, of Swinton, near Manchester. Simon Fraser of Liverpool, with his vast background of union experience, described Chloride Batteries to me in December 1976 as 'one of the happiest of factories'. He described management's efforts to achieve good working relationships with the unions there as 'absolutely fascinating'. Derrick George, for fourteen years TGWU convener at Chloride, is respected by all, including management and trade unionists at Chloride, but he would not quite agree with Simon Fraser. The word 'participation' is constantly on his tongue, and he was responsible in 1968, with the other members of the Shop Stewards' Committee of Chloride, for a definition in detail of 'what we mean by participation'. The list of demands was duly presented to Chloride. It read as follows:

1. Being involved in all important decision-making before it happens, not after.

2. To be involved in other decisions, not just Manufacturing Division.

3. To be able to have high level talks when either shop floor or management deem it necessary.

4. To be educated in the workings of other divisions, education being important to better industrial relations.

5. For better industrial relations to know the plan for loading of factory (what it means?). To be involved in the decisions about the load and to see the best way for the labour force to be used (i.e. new methods, safety, new machinery, space, etc.).

6. To be able to get information when we ask for it, in the manner in which we ask for it.

7. All information to be passed on to us – not just when it suits management to tell us.

8. That both shop floor and management accept correct information and make decisions accordingly.

9. When it is agreed, the policy of the shop floor and management on participation for a proper communications system to be passed down to all management personnel.

10. All the above is the shop floor's interpretation of participation in the broadest sense, which will lead to better industrial relations and a more sound and prosperous wage structure.

Here, then, in 1968, is a fascinating demand for participation, in the sense of the maximum of communication from management to the work force and for involvement in decision-making. It represents an itch to be in the know and to have a management committed to working with the shop stewards. Chloride duly accepted the demand for this sort of participation. However, after both 1968 and Simon Fraser's 1976 tribute to industrial relations at Chloride, there occurred the nine weeks' strike of 1977. Since then, Derrick George tells me, he would add to the list of demands in the name of participation two further items: that the information given by management should be 'full' information, and that all decisions should be made jointly by management and union representatives. The changes in wording are slight, but the significance considerable. There has been a hardening of attitudes.

Let us look hard at Derrick George, a big man in every way. As convener he has an office and a telephone. Secretarial assistance is available if required. At one time he succeeded in persuading all workers at Chloride Batteries to work for 'parity', for the same wage. In defending this, he would say to the young: 'You'll be forty some day. Some day you'll be sixty. You won't want your wage to come down because you're older then.' Of the toilet cleaner he said to all that he was doing a very important job, not at all one meriting a lower wage. 'We all belong,' he said. He puts men into their jobs, he tells me. He explains that there is an understanding: 'Derrick, you run the shop floor.' He tries to do so, giving the young men the harder jobs. He says that he 'places' 95% of the men. He thinks that he ought to place the other 5%. He believes he should recruit the whole force. He is sure that he knows what is needed, that he knows where each man should go. Management, he complains, is always changing; managers are looking over their shoulders for better jobs; middle management loses heart with age (he says). He himself stays on, is re-elected to office every two years. If he cannot get a decision from floor management, he says to me, he steps over it, goes straight to the General Manager. Derrick is, of course, a union man, on the union side. Yet he is in management also, helping with his great personality and influence to organize and run the shop floor (and more than the shop floor) at Chloride. He has taken upon himself a managemental role, and Chloride has wisely accepted that beneficial assumption of managemental authority. He believes that, at Chloride at least, foremen are unnecessary. Shop stewards, he says, could do the job.

Well and good. Yet we must ask how much of the real responsibility of management is the good convener capable of taking? To what extent is he able to see and face up to the fact that hard work has to be done to produce effectively, to compete effectively, to keep the prices of Chloride batteries sufficiently low so that they will sell? It is these hard facts of economic and commercial life that management has to deal with, and it is just these hard facts that the best of unionists on the shop floor (and elsewhere) sometimes (but by no means always) seem unable or unwilling to deal with. The fault here lies in our inadequate education system, which offers no real preparation for the economic facts of life. And yet in some areas of industry, workers (shop stewards especially) can and do assist in much of the work of management. Amongst the stewards are some highly intelligent men and women, more capable and more intelligent than many foremen and many of those higher in management. However, they will not 'cross over', accept promotion to management proper. It is wastage, a shame for industry, if their real capacity for management cannot in some way be employed in managemental function, albeit from the shop floor.

As to the company's response to Derrick's new demands, a

spokesman tells me that joint decision-making for all decisions is 'out'. It would be unacceptable to the majority of managements, as it would be unsought by the majority of unions. Management believes that there is some expertise, some specialized capacity in managing. There would be many conveners in this country who would tell Derrick that he must accept that. He has been promised and given involvement with management in decisions concerning the load and the labour force on the shop floor. He has been promised 'full information' (but claims that he does not receive it). Trade unionism is powerful at Chloride Batteries, and it is generally agreed that conditions are good. The company is in competition now (as it was not a few years ago) with a number of other companies producing batteries, and has to take care that it is not priced out of the market. The company, which has to cope with strong competition from outside, has also to deal with suspicion from its own workers. It has had to put over to its workers as hard as it can the need to increase productivity in order to stay in the market. It does not seem to have been able to convince. Perhaps its task might have been less difficult if there had been fewer changes in management. During Derrick's time, the spokesman for the company admits, there have certainly been many such changes. The fact remains that here is a company which is recognized to have enlightened management of a high calibre and yet one which seems unable to convince the union leaders of the urgent economic need to be more competitive. This is a serious and (sadly) a typical problem in modern British industry.

Elsewhere in this book suggestions are made to explain how it is that there can be a non-meeting of minds amongst decent men of good will on the two sides of industry. Here one can only plead for patience and perseverance, for a relentless searching of people in close contact with one another for some new way of breaking into what seem to be the closed minds on the other side, of finding some inlet through the mental barriers which separate. Derrick George has said that he cares for the future of Chloride Batteries. He is one of many amongst the Chloride workers who 'would like his sons to come here'. There is a minimum basic involvement, and on this it ought to be possible to build growing understanding.

Sometimes, as we shall see a little later in this chapter, with the best will in the world, the communications which management wishes to be 'full' just do not happen. Not all management realizes the seriousness of such failure when it occurs. The Prince of Wales chose to speak out on this subject at a luncheon on 21 February

1979. It was a carefully prepared speech, based on his own recent experiences. According to BBC TV News, addressing his audience with care and deliberation he said: 'I discovered during my recent visits that the problem of communication between management and shop floor frequently stems from a failure of communications *within* management. When front line managers are accused of poor communications the truth is that they cannot communicate because they don't know much themselves. . . I haven't the slightest hesitation in making the observation that much of British management doesn't seem to understand the importance of the human factor in the whole process.' The BBC reported that the Chairman of the Institute of Directors called the Prince's remarks 'a pity'; the late Director-General of the CBI attributed them to inexperience; Sir Richard Marsh described them as 'daft'. Yet a former personnel director explained to me how such failures do sometimes happen. The General Manager, he said, must communicate to his factory managers, the factory managers to the plant managers, the plant managers to first-line supervision. Suddenly, however, up comes a very important meeting or conference, and someone has to be away. As a result, there is delay in the passing on of information. There is a temporary break in the line of communication. The first the workers hear of the news is from their shop steward, who has obtained it from his convener, who got it straight from the General Manager. It has not come to the hourly-paid workers quite as top management meant it to come. Then management is accused of not communicating. These things happen. They ought not to happen and would not happen if management were trained in the vital importance of communicating properly.

Later in the year, the late Sir John Methven, at the CBI National Conference of 1979 in Birmingham, declared that he wanted to talk to his fellow industrialists about the 'positive side' of relationships, 'about communicating, about winning hearts and minds, and about management's responsibilities'. 'From whom,' he added, 'are workers, going to get information about their own firm, their own employment, which is credible?' 'We cannot,' he went on, 'we must not, leave it to anyone else but ourselves. *We*, managers, must tell them.' He quoted a recent CBI survey which 'showed that less than half of the 450 companies surveyed had regular meetings between management and employees to discuss business performance *or for any other purpose*. This is a shocking figure. Sir John was echoing the challenge of his own (CBI) President at the same conference: 'My main message today, my Lords, Ladies and Gentlemen, is – let us tune-in to communications, in depth and repetitive terms in a way that we have never tuned-in before.' How much must be lacking if leaders of industry are impelled to appeal publicly in this tone to their fellow industrialists.

Under the 1975 Employment Protection Act, there are now legal requirements. The law on disclosure of information to trade unions for collective bargaining purposes is set out in sections 17 to 21 of the Act. It requires an employer to disclose upon request all information about his business or the business of an associated employer without which trade union representatives would be impeded to a material extent in collective bargaining and which it would be good industrial relations practice to disclose. The Advisory Conciliation and Arbitration Service issues a Code of Practice[7] which came into effect under the Act on 22 August 1977. The Act, says the Code, places on the employer a general duty to disclose at all stages of negotiation information requested by representatives of 'independent trade unions'. The employer is not obliged to disclose anything which would impose injury on the undertaking 'for reasons other than its effect on collective bargaining'. This is slightly more felicitously worded than the Leyland Cars *Employee Communication* report of 1977, which said with considerable haughtiness that 'it is not possible or desirable that every employee should know everything about the company'. Under the Code of Practice a trade union denied information may appeal to the Central Arbitration Committee. If the complaint is upheld by the Committee, the employer is obliged to disclose the information. The Code states that the sort of information which a union has the right to request and obtain concerns the principles and structure of payment systems, conditions of service, matters concerning employment, including investment plans, details of productivity, sales and orders, return on capital invested, cost structures, profits, loans, and government assistance. The list is reasonably comprehensive.

If Sir John Methven's challenge to management is to be taken up, if Derrick George's post-1968 demand is to be favourably answered, more than the legal minimum Code of Practice quantity of information needs to be conceded by management to its colleagues in the work force. While the dull are content to plod on with indifference, intelligent men and women burn to know more about that business in which they are involved and upon which their futures and their families' are dependent. The fact that the CBI has produced 'an important guide for senior management on employee communication in industry' (called *Communication with People at Work*) suggests that wise management is not satisfied with present practice. In the CBI's *Guidelines for Action on Employee Involvement*, the authors say: 'Managers and supervisors must be held accountable for communicating with their own teams, with active board commitment to providing information on a regular basis. This commitment must be permanent – and seen to be so.' They add that an 'essential requirement is that managers operate their own channels through which they speak regularly to all employees *as employees*'. Provision for communication, they go on to say, should be on a regular and systematic basis. 'Employees need to know about plans and issues which are of vital importance to the firm,' they write, adding that the company's financial position needs to be explained regularly. This, they say, is best done by senior managers explaining it face to face.

Communication to the workers ought to be as clear in meaning and as genuinely frank as circumstances permit. In September 1961, at the critical stage of a dispute between Mount Isa Mines in North Queensland and its work force, the company circulated to the miners an economic tract in its defence which, in my opinion, required an economist to interpret. It was not read. A former Yorkshire father of the chapel in a branch of SLADE (The Society of Lithographic Artists, Designers and Engravers) told me how his union was obliged to employ an accountant to explain to the members the meaning of the figures supplied by management. There are ways of communicating which improve relationships and ways which diminish them. Geoff, the young communist shop steward of chapter 5, claims that John, the senior shop steward of the same chapter, went into the company participation scheme in the hope of a real share of information as well as of a share in decision-making. He declares that John found himself up against management which did indeed give information, but which defined what it gave as confidential. 'You can't use that information,' he said that the company told John. 'You can't trust workers to keep a secret,' they said. It is, however, a fact that workers can keep secrets if they believe that it is in the common interest for them to do so, and provided that management has won their confidence. Lord Mountbatten, in his SE Asia command between 1943 and 1945, put into practice his faith that, if you took ordinary men into your confidence and told them that their safety depended upon their respect for that confidence, they would not fail you (or fail themselves). I saw the method work as we re-entered Japanese-held Burma in 1944.

In the Greene King Breweries of today there are discussion groups, held quarterly, during company time. These are organized on a departmental basis, and all who work in the department are expected to attend. 'A good many do,' says a shop steward. At the discussion groups, any subject concerning what is done in the brewery may be brought up. Any ideas which might benefit the work or the workers can be aired. Management sometimes takes advantage of the meeting to explain some aspect of company policy and a representative of management is always present. When questions are asked which he himself is unable to answer at the time, he promises an answer. This answer is posted up for all to see before the next meeting of the discussion group. 'This company,' says a shop steward, 'believes in the discussion groups.' They are genuine means of communication.

There is a need for managers not only to listen to their own CBI, but to try to realize how important to a live work force communications really are. It is a fact which needs to be frankly and honestly faced that for the work force information is important because it strengthens its bargaining position. On the other hand, where there are financial difficulties which are plainly and honestly explained, management will often find not only understanding but restraint from its work force. If the thirteen-week steel strike of early 1980 appeared to be an exception to this 'rule' there were also exceptional circumstances attached to this lamentable dispute in a nationalized industry. Management, of course, may become exasperated with demands which appear to it to be quite unreasonable. Yet the demands remain and must be treated patiently and reasonably. The EETPU in its *Shop Stewards Handbook* assures its shop-floor leaders that 'good communications are the key to understanding and involvement'. It goes on: 'It is a key part of your role to ensure that you are an effective communicator.' In many places, in many ways, and at various times, unions plead with management for knowledge of future plans for companies and plants, for news of prospects. Given the basic concern of the employee for his job security, that employee cannot fail to be concerned with the future of the firm on which that security depends. In a Lancashire firm in December 1976 senior shop stewards were scarcely able to think or talk to me of anything except 'the injustice' of the fact that management allegedly knew the details of the proposals for future close-downs, while the stewards, the representatives of the workers, were denied that knowledge.

In the report already referred to of the British Leyland Sub-Committee on *Employee Communication*, the case for 'a strategy' of communication to the workers was clearly laid down. The report was endorsed by the Leyland Cars Joint Management Council. The policy for Leyland Cars was stated emphatically to be one of 'an open and participative style of management', with the involvement of employees . . . through effective employee communication, and with the exchange of information and ideas between all levels of employees. The company pledged itself to the maximum of downward communication and to the encouragement of the receipt and use of ideas from all levels of employees. There were to be monthly briefings to all members of management, and opportunity for the regular briefing of employees. 'Line supervision,' it said, 'and union representatives' were to be 'well informed', and line supervision was to be adequately supported in its responsibilities for work place communication. There were to be adequate formal channels for the feedback of response and queries. Local 'Employee Communication Officers' were continually to review the effectiveness of local systems of communications and to recommend improvements. Dermot Carroll of Cowley, a member of the company's Participation Committee, described the system to me as 'fantastic'.

There are, however, others at Cowley who disagree on the subject of the efficacy of the system of communications. A former EETPU steward instances as a failure in communications the company's declaration of inability to pay (in February 1979) the extra which would bring about parity amongst the skilled workers through BL, provided that productivity reached an agreed level. He declares that the failure in productivity must have been obvious to management before the disappointing decision not to pay was made. If this developing failure had been communicated to the unions, he believes that the workers would have been willing and able to improve production. He says that management just made a bald statement: 'We haven't got enough money; you haven't generated enough production; we cannot pay you parity.' He says, shaking his head, that they do not look hard at the problem. 'They must have known,' he says, 'that the situation was going to come up. They should have come to the trade unions earlier and said, "Look, we've been running behind. We're not producing enough. How about putting the line speed up on a temporary basis and working without extra labour on the tracks so that you're producing more and picking up the vehicles you've lost and not increasing the staff that's producing them?" ' He goes on with despair rather than bitterness: 'That is the way we could have picked up our lost production. But they never came to us with that offer. On the day the parity pay was due, they just said: "Sorry, lads, you haven't done enough." . . . They gave no warning to us.' He says again: 'They must have known the thing was going wrong. December's figures were wavering, January's were a disaster. If they are intelligent men, they must have seen how matters were going.' Another Cowley worker, a mature man, the father of three teenage children, reports: 'You don't hear anything unless you read the *Oxford Mail*.'

Mr John Garnett, Director of the Industrial Society, in his *Manager's Responsibility for Communication*, declares that communication matters 'because failures in communication are costly'. He adds that 'out of 35 stoppages in a large organization 18 were due to failure of communication'. In the Industrial Society's *Participation – The Proven Code*, the author, John Wates, reminds managers of what the CBI has told them: that it is for management, not for shop stewards, to explain management's policies to workers. He goes on to affirm that in 'realistic participation', the distribution of 'relevant information' is not enough; it is in fact 'fundamental' for 'management to be aware of, and to take into account, the views and wishes of employees expressed through their representatives, *prior* to making decisions'. Joe Roeber, in his account of the initiation and development of the 'Weekly Staff Agreement' between employers and unions in ICI, writes both of the difficulties and of the benefits, as 'total managerial authority' was succeeded by a system of consultation. He quotes Mr Robin Paul, later to be works manager at ICI's Castner-Kellner works in Cheshire, on the 'Weekly Staff Agreement' as it worked out: 'The huge benefit on the management side was of forcing a complete change in the relationship with work people . . . they had a dialogue and a day-to-day relationship with their weekly staff in which the comments on the job were flowing up just as naturally as down . . . so that the habit of questioning whether something was necessary, or whether the right instruction had been given was established in the factory. Out of this we led into the regular communications meeting where every operator has the opportunity to discuss his work with management and supervision.'[8]

Dr Kevin Hawkins makes an interesting distinction between what he calls 'task-centred' and what he calls 'power-centred' participation.[9] 'Task-centred' participation means the partial or full control of the workers over the way in which their allotted task is performed. The Government, the TUC and the CBI contributed in 1975 to the drawing up of the report of the Tripart Steering Group on job satisfaction. It made a series of practical proposals for shop-floor participation (as opposed to policy-making at board level). It came out in favour of autonomous work groups, which give workers a share in decision-making in the details of their work, 'discretion' (as the report says) 'for planning and organizing work among themselves'. The autonomous work group has its objective, and goes about the means of achieving it in its own way. 'Group working,' says the report, 'reflecting various degrees of autonomy, provides a framework for building closely-knit teams, and for this reason is more likely to fulfil people's needs. Where the autonomy of the group is progressively increased as they demonstrate their willingness and capacity to accept it, there is considerable evidence to show that many people respond readily to this type of organization.' The report goes on to say that where there are to be changes in work organization, 'everyone who will be affected by the changes should be involved in planning the change programme'. Such changes, it says, 'imply a managemental style with less emphasis on control, checking and the maintenance of systems, and sensitive enough to cope with the more dynamic and complicated systems which cover change'.[10] One must bear in mind that the scope for experiments of this kind is to some extent limited by the developing technology which enables one man and a machine to achieve what was previously the work of a group. It is interesting that the Swedish experience, where, it is claimed at Kalmar, human work groups have taken over from the mechanical line,[11] has not convinced the British or German or French or Italian car industries that it would be economic to imitate it. Nor has the system been adopted at the vast Soviet Togliattigrad car plant (visited by John in 1977). Neither at Kalmar itself have the 'human work groups' solved the problem of absenteeism.

Power-centred participation may meet a deeper need. Hawkins quotes from *Workers' Participation in Management in Britain* to define power-centred participation as 'extending the bargaining power of the workers within the enterprise and . . . making managerial decision-makers more accountable either to the unions or more directly to the workers'.[12] This implies that workers are, in certain circumstances, to have some degree of control over the decisions which management makes. Hawkins develops a case for just this, if the worker is to become truly 'involved'.[13] In some cases, there seems no other answer to the seemingly utter 'non-involvement' of the worker. The Finniston *Report* describes this non-involvement of the workers as 'an uninterested attitude to the company which employs them' and which is for them simply a source of weekly income.[14] Some in management may hold that workers' power-centred participation is unacceptable; others may come to see it as a price well worth paying for workers' involvement. The CBI and many of its members have to face up to the hard fact that in some units of industry neither good communications nor the maximum of consultation is enough. Some have already faced up to it. In some places at least, where workers and their leaders are ready for it, there has to be a share in decision-making, a share in managemental responsibility itself. With increase of involvement, there could be increase of productivity.

Fergus Panton, a management school consultant, writing for the Working Together Campaign (of employers, managers and trade unionists), declares that there is likely to be no long-term improvement in employee involvement until discussion groups and project teams recruited from both sides are set up throughout industry. These, he says, are to analyse the environment and the organization, to agree on policy guide-lines, to examine and develop practices and procedures, and to monitor results.[15] Surely he is basically right, so long as this programme is not treated as necessary in every detail for every unit of industry. Yet more is needed in many units of industry than Fergus Panton suggests. We shall not get the maximum of involvement, nor will justice be rendered to all capable of responsibility, until participation is seen sometimes at least to involve much more than communication and consultation.

Dr Hawkins maintains his point. He writes that 'some recent research suggests that there is a considerable demand by workers for more influence over decisions affecting their jobs'.[16] This is a vital point for the worker, not an easy one for the professional man to comprehend. He has relative security, the worker has not. The Bullock Commission's report on *Industrial Democracy* states that 'the purely consultative system, where it is clearly understood that, however much influence those consulted may have, any decisions taken are those of management, is becoming less common. Consultation is being developed to the point where those consulted have a *de facto* power of veto over certain actions of management.'[17] A power of veto is a big step into managerial responsibility. This kind of thinking is not easy for the more traditional type of management to accept. Yet it may be the way towards workers' involvement, the way towards productivity, towards industrial salvation.

The Hon. G. H. Wilson, Joint Managing Director of the Delta Group, is open-minded. He says to me with frankness that 'management has no divine right, or any sort of right, to manage'. On the other hand, he goes on, management has a duty to use its capacity, its experience and its expertise. He says that his group is constantly working to improve the system of decision-making. His group's Report for 1977 stated that there was amongst its workers 'a growing realization of the need for higher productivity if the full potential of our recent investment in heavy capital plant is to be realized and reflected in lower costs'. It asserts that it 'endeavours to involve employees in the decision-making processes to the maximum practicable extent'. That is saying a great deal. There seemed to me to be managemental sincerity in all this.

We have entered territory in which researchers (and others) must tread delicately, where there are strong feelings on both sides. Yet there is room for unprejudiced experiment by men of good will. As long ago as the 1960s, the Glacier Metal Company in its *Policy Document* of 1965 appeared to be developing a far-reaching extension of participation. It spoke of a 'legislative system', whereby 'policies shall be determined by unanimous agreement at council meetings (if it should be the desire of members in 'designated areas' to form such councils). The councils (if and when formed) were 'to determine by unanimous agreement . . . legislative policies which best meet the requirements of the company and of the members of the operating organizations'. Its former Chief Executive, Lord (Wilfred) Brown, founded in 1961 the Glacier Institute of Management. In its statement about itself the Institute described 'co-determination' as a means of achieving a higher degree of participation by employees. Co-determination gave employees the direct right to appoint their own members of the directing body, thus giving them 'a more immediate control of executive activities'. The statement went on to say that in such a directing body, 'it is more likely . . . that it will be tacitly accepted that representatives of both factions have to agree to proposals before they are duly authorized'. However, this is not quite how the system now works. At the end of the 1970s there was at the Glacier Metal Company, Alperton, a Works Committee for the London factories. It comprises elected representatives of both hourly-paid workers and staff from the offices, with charge-hands, foremen and representatives of middle management. It meets monthly, normally for three and a half hours, on the first Tuesday of each month. The Committee is about thirty strong, and its members go back to their constituents to report before making a decision. There is also a Works Council, and it needs to be made clear that the Works Council (on which sit a 'Management Member' appointed by the Chief Executive, as well as a representative of management higher in the hierarchy than any on the Works Committee) has a clear right of veto over decisions of the Works Committee. The Personnel Director at Alperton was emphatic to me on this point.

The history of the evolution and development of Lord Brown's idea and experiments at Glacier Metal is fascinating and significant. The system does not seem to have developed quite as Lord Brown intended. Yet it seemed to me at Alperton that an important step forward in industrial relations had been made in the sense that there was there a clear definition of the 'determining manager', of the person present and available with authority to make decisions. Indeed in the case of the annual pay settlement, the determining manager for that purpose called on the union convener while I was sitting in his office. The convener promised to return the call; he had not far to go. It seemed that the pay settlement was 'in the bag.' I had found at Alperton something quite different from what I had been led to expect. John Power, himself a senior shop steward and convener, pleads for the location of 'determining management . . . at as low a level as possible in the interest of industrial relations'. He writes (in a privately circulated paper): 'Shop stewards, senior shop stewards, managers and industrial relations men are constantly together. In the course of their debates, pragmatical solutions emerge in many cases. I cannot describe to you the number of times I have reached satisfactory arrangements with members of management.' That of course, depended upon members of management with authority being present and available.

To return to the possibility of workers having a real share in the responsibility of decision-making, let us begin by considering in what ways workers are already sharing in management and to what extent this is capable of becoming more common without loss of industrial efficiency. Let us go on to take the plunge boldly and ask managers to be wise enough to see if they cannot make use for community's and production's sake of the union groups in their midst. Professor Peter Drucker has referred to research which shows that sometimes in industrial enterprises 'there is an informal social organization of the workers' which already is 'in management' (along with supervisory and managerial personnel).[18] He goes on: 'It is this informal organization rather than management which actually determines rates of output, standards, job classification, and job content.' However much management must manage, it is the shop steward who is often an unofficial, more or less unrecognized member of management, in so far as he plays a significant part in the deployment and organization of labour. The foremen's strikes at Ford's and BL during 1978 showed how competently shop stewards could at least temporarily take over the supervisory duties in some plants.

Dr Alan Fox writes that 'management has to face the fact that there are sources of leadership and focuses of loyalty outside management within industry, and that it must share its leadership if it is to be realistic'.[19] If it is prepared to do so, it may help to bring out in union leaders capacity which could be of great service in industry. Let anti-union management ask itself seriously where large-scale industry would be without trade unions to assist it in the organization of its labour force. BL in 1980 wants its production of cars at its Longbridge plant to grow by an extra 342,000 cars a year from new equipment using 70% fewer workers and on only one shift a day. It has invested £285 million there, and one half of Britain's total of industrial robots is to be found in one Longbridge building.[20] It will be possible to weld and assemble a complete car body every 42 seconds; 38 men are needed to make car bodies compared with 138 in a conventional plant.[21] Obviously there have to be changes in working practices. If these were to be attempted without being explained to the leaders of organized groups of workers (the unions) there would be chaos. Mr Ray Horrocks, the combative Managing Director of Austin Morris, was quoted on ITV News on 21 April 1980 as saying very loudly and clearly: 'Without the trade unions, there is no way we could run BL Cars.' This is the kind of highly significant statement that does not usually get into the papers. What did get into the papers was the statement of the TGWU leader, Mr Moss Evans, who said that the unions and particularly the shop stewards would still have some say in manning levels, the speed of the line and even trips to the toilet. He said that the unions had got the management to recognize the important function of the shop steward.[22] If this is true, it seems a little late in the industrial day.

In studying the capacity of union men to share in management, one cannot completely ignore the inventive ingenuity of the Lucas Aerospace 'Combine Shop Stewards Committee'. After men had been threatened by Lucas Aerospace with redundancy in the 1960s, these shop stewards worked out and produced plans for the production of 150 'socially useful' products which, they claimed, could be made with the existing tools and skills available at Lucas Aerospace. These proposals were set out in 1500 printed pages, published in 1976. They included the production of aids for people handicapped by spina bifida, solar collecting equipment, power packs, road-rail vehicles and 'telearchic' devices mimicking the motions of a human being. There was an electrically-powered vehicle in which a small petrol engine drove a generator. This topped up the batteries, and these supplied power to the electric motor which drove the transmission. It was reckoned that the combination would reduce both fuel consumption and air pollution, and it would also be noiseless. From Sweden, from Australia, from Japan and elsewhere, came inquiries about the Shop Stewards Committee *Corporate Plan*. While Lucas's was at first unwilling to take these proposals seriously, the Open University and Toyota and Bosch all showed practical concern for them. The combine initially failed to win support from its own unions; it was an unofficial body. It represented at first, as the stewards admitted, a challenge to managemental prerogatives. It demanded a real shift in power to the workers. Nevertheless, the company had to admit that none of the proposals was technically impractical. Mick Young, one of the Combine Committee, suggested to a group of us at Slough on 12 September 1979 that the stewards concerned were men of experience capable of growth in wisdom and in a spirit of co-operation. We were prepared to believe him.

As time went on, the militancy and the list of proposed products altered. These products were now to be called 'alternative' rather than 'socially useful'. As the result of a modified document produced in 1979, and owing to new support from the TUC, the Labour Party and the Government, a Products Committee of Lucas Industries was formed, to include Combine Committee shop stewards, trade union officials, and representatives of management and of the Department of Industry. The committee has been meeting regularly and taking the proposals seriously. *Management*

Today, in commenting unfavourably on the plan, could not withhold the admiring comment that 'the ingenuity that went into this assemblage, and the genuine altruism apparent in its frequent regard to social utility are beyond question'. The same article explained why management had originally regarded the proposals from this unofficial committee with considerable suspicion.[23] The fact remained that the inventiveness and perseverance, as well as the adaptibility of the stewards had come to be recognized.

For those unaccustomed to think of shop stewards as men concerned with productivity, it might be of interest to read the report of a conference organized over the week-end of 27–28 October 1979 for fifty active members of trade unions. It was held in Cumbria under the auspices of the Jim Conway Foundation and dealt with *Technology and Change in Industry*. A trade union official addressing the conference declared that unionists 'should be fighting for new technology'. The whole conference was absorbed in the attempt to grasp the 'potential benefit of microelectric technology'. All the groups at the conference were unanimous in finding that there was 'an inevitable need to develop new skills, and that the use of "robotics" would create new jobs'.[24] Here surely was some constructive, even daring, thinking on the part of ordinary trade unionists. At another Jim Conway Foundation conference a month later, a leading speaker called on union men to 'accept and stimulate technical change', to 'make themselves efficient'.

The Lucas Aerospace Combine leaders were stewards from the shop floor. They were keen union men, at first unsupported by their national leaders. Nevertheless, the union was (and is) to such men part of their identity. To them it does not mean some body at union headquarters, but rather the union where they know it, in its reality on the shop floor. It is this reality commanding loyalty that industrialists (and others) seem at times to find incomprehensible, perhaps because they think of 'the unions' in terms of national figures appearing on television screens. The concept of loyalty to a union is particularly difficult for some to accept after the 'winter of discontent' and the industrial action amongst many in the public service unions. Employers sigh for a loyalty to the firm which (it is said) provides workers with their living. Surely, they claim, there should be an overriding loyalty to that firm with whose welfare the worker's well-being is inevitably bound up. In a country of sport and the sporting tradition, the industrialist appeals for a 'united side', a 'team spirit', amongst 'his' workers. At the CBI National Conference of 1979, the President, Sir John Hedley Greenborough, made this almost predictable appeal:

> I made a plea at our first Conference, and in our second, to get away from the constant reference to 'both sides of industry' and talk, instead, about a united industrial team. But my plea has gone unheeded. The media, Cabinet Ministers, the Opposition, and plenty of people in the CBI, still go on talking about consulting 'both sides of industry'. As long as we go on saying this, we will perpetuate the adversary concept. I am not a great reader of Hansard, nor have I ever attended a Parliamentary debate on national defence, but I'm pretty sure that I am right when I say that never once, in any such debates, has anybody ever said that they have "consulted both sides of the Navy, or both sides of the Army". Yet what do we look for, in the Army and the Navy, and what have we got? Effective fighting forces, admittedly in defence terms. What are we looking for in industry? Also an effective fighting force but in our case, in aggressive terms, a force that can take on the best of our international competitors and knock the hell out of them!! . . . What are we looking for at the end of the day? As I see it, in a free society working in a mixed economy, we want total commitment from all those who work in a company, to the prosperity of that company. That is their prime loyalty, or should be their prime loyalty, and this in no way is downgrading the role of the trade union leaders who, I have already suggested at national level, should be rewarded substantially. It means that the prime loyalty of unionized employees to the company is supported by a strong but secondary loyalty to the union that looks after their collective interests . . . I remember, some years ago, discussing the subject of loyalty with a national trade union personality well known in those days. It was about unionized labour in my own company, and he was saying to me: 'John, my lads would do this – or would not do that', and I said to him (let him be nameless, but let's just refer to him as Jack), 'For two minutes, and for no longer, could I just refer to these chaps as *my* lads? You see I have what you may think is an old-fashioned view about this. But I recruit them and I train them, and I pay them and I develop them, and I promote them, and I retire them and I pension them, and I even have a pensioners' liaison organization that goes to see them after

they've finished working for us, and in my old-fashioned way I believe that they, in their eyes, become *your* lads when I appear to be letting them down!' As you will readily appreciate we did not reach a consensus view on this.

It was brave, pathetic, utterly uncomprehending.

Gently, firmly, I plead with Sir John and others: you are asking for what you cannot have for the asking. Do not talk to men or of men like this. Prime loyalty goes where the heart lies, and normally the worker's heart goes to the union where he knows and is known as nowhere else. This is a hard fact for the employer to face, but he must deal with reality not fantasy. It simply is not good enough to be a good employer and to appeal for filial devotion. It is no help to compare an industry or a unit of an industry with a team and to ask for an appropriate spirit. In a team one can appeal to the individual player to sacrifice his personal success in favour of that of the team. In industry one cannot ask the worker to sacrifice adequate wages and conditions; he needs them for his life's and family's sake. Only in the minds (and sometimes on the tongues) of 'leaders of industry' out of touch with workers can such an appeal be made and 'unresponsive' workers be blamed for not risking their living. Sometimes (but not always) in industry, conflicting interests make men not a team but two hostile sides. This is no matter of mere perversity, but one to be comprehended and sensitively handled and eventually out-grown.

Management has to face up frankly and honestly to the facts of economic life. Peter Drucker wrote that management, on behalf of the employer and in its own interest, must aim at profit-making. He went on: 'The main function and purpose of the enterprise is the production of goods, not the governance of men. Its governmental authority over men must always be subordinated to its economic performance and responsibility. . . Hence it can never be discharged primarily in the interest of those over whom the enterprise rules.' He added that as far as the worker is concerned, the management in the government-owned enterprise of a socialist state is fully as much 'management' as if the enterprise were personally owned by J. P. Morgan and operated for his exclusive benefit.[25] This must be squarely faced and rationally accepted. Management has profit-making as its prime aim, however benevolent and sensitive it may be to its workers' needs. The workers have their prime aims too: to keep their jobs, 'to lead a civilized life', 'to pay the electricity bills'. In days of threatened job security, the ensuring of all this is sometimes an agonizing task.

In the midst of such anxieties, the strongest of workers looks around for an ally. Behind the worker is the union. The union gives him what he most needs: a sense of security. Without the bastion of assured union support, there is the great risk of social oblivion, 'of being excluded, disregarded, of being made to feel of no value . . . neglected and disparaged'.[26] But he knows that the union is with him, always there. 'Unions,' says *The Economist*, 'are credited with defending their members' interests . . . workers flock to join them.'[27]

Between 1966 and 1976 trade union membership in Britain increased by 20%, by no means an insignificant figure. Kevin Hawkins quotes Daniel's and McIntosh's *Right to Manage?*, to show that the worker feels that his chance of personal advancement in status and earnings lies in the advancement of the group of which he is a member.[28] This may represent no Elizabethan spirit of personal enterprise, but it is a fact of modern working life. The union is a worker's club, his church.

Management has to see that loyalty to the company before loyalty to the union cannot be demanded of workers who feel deeply within themselves their commitments to their unions and to their fellow-unionists and dare not and will not dispense with them. A young steel worker, sad to be on strike in March 1980, spoke of what he felt: 'You've got to go with your union, haven't you? You've got to stick together, haven't you?' No fulminations by the CBI, no parliamentary legislation, can take away this kind of union 'power' over union members. Management has to cope. Men can be won, but they cannot be bullied out of union loyalties. Management must try to forget the long-ago battles for union rights. It ought to learn to live with much of the legacy of Labour-dominated Parliaments. It has to forgo the sterile luxury of bitterness towards those unions to which its men for the most part proudly belong. If management is hostile in principle to the unions, relations with its men will be strained before they begin to happen. In fact, discerning management realizes that within a factory or a plant there are various interests at work. Let management do all it can by just treatment to cause employees to identify with their companies. Let 'family spirit' grow, in factories where workers find fellowship and care and which they can recommend to their children. Yet management changes, as workers know. With change of management, there is sometimes change of spirit. The union remains. The union appears to be unchanging. A ready-made tradition of support and fellowship seems to exist and persist.

Let management try to understand the haunting spectre of redundancy as it stalks in the worker's mind. Redundancy may lead to unemployment. Let management have no illusion that unemployment, with all the leisure it implies, is a pleasurable prospect in the worker's mind. It is not so. 'To be unemployed in your home town – that destroys your soul,' said a young north-country worker on BBC Television on 1 February 1980. People talk of the abuse of social security benefits, but the statistics of the Supplementary Benefits Commission show that when men become unemployed there is normally a cut of over 40% in their income. The Shadow Education Secretary said in the House of Commons on 21 January of the same year that it does not take opinion polls in *The Times* or anywhere else to prove that 100% of trade unionists and other workers like to have jobs. Rightly or wrongly, the union man believes that the union protects him against unemployment. The manager may choose to think that the unions (with all their strikes) may be the main cause of workers' unemployment. But the worker does not see the union in this light at all. Nothing is likely to persuade him to the contrary. He often feels insecure, within a complex of which he understands little except for the minutiae of his job. He may lose that job. I spoke recently to a young man who had applied for an appointment (and not obtained it). Trying to help, I asked him what he was. He replied, without cynicism or bitterness, that he was nothing. It was not a complaint, but merely what seemed to him to be fact. In the awful nothingness of redundancy, or in the fear of it, the union is there. At least the union, if nobody else, cares. As Peter Berger, the sociologist, writes: 'Any historical society is an order, a protective structure of meaning, erected in the face of chaos. Within this order . . . the life of the individual makes sense.' The individual needs to be within ordered structure.

Management must not be grudging in its acceptance of the right of unions to exist and to influence their members. Berger describes 'a fundamental proposition of the sociology of knowledge' to the effect that 'we obtain our notions originally from other human beings, and these notions continue to be plausible to us in a very large measure because others continue to affirm them'.[29] Not many persons do very much thinking for themselves. Berger mentions the well-known statement of Gabriel Le Bras to the effect that Catholics cease to practise Catholicism as soon as they reach a certain Paris railway station. The union provides the environment in which many workers grow up and mature; in it inevitably they develop their industrial concepts. There is no reason why men who accept ideas from the union should *ipso facto* be anti-management in mind. It is just that they are pro-union. Men can grow, and learn, and change their minds. With wise management and with intercourse between management and workers, there may well be acceptance of management's ideas sometimes in addition to those of the union, occasionally in place of them. Where there is community, community ideas will grow among men. A TGWU shop steward in an East Anglian brewery wrote to me in 1979 of 'wonderful relations', of a management 'always ready to sit round the table'. He added, however that 'good will is double-edged, and that in turn reflects on the splendid 99% membership that our union has'. Good relations and loyal union membership can and do co-exist. Management needs to accept with good will the pluralism which unions incarnate. There is room for more than one loyalty in industry. The same shop steward writes almost with affection of the brewery's long-standing 'splendid' record of 'not laying people off'. 'Redundancy,' he writes, 'is a word seldom if ever used.' Let management listen thoughtfully to that.

Sometimes, of course, there have to be redundancies. Then, and at other times too, there may well be a clash of loyalties. This is in the nature of things. It need not be the end of relationships, but rather one of a series of natural reactions which reasonable men who know one another can reasonably settle. If there has to be debate, disagreement, struggle, there need not be bitterness. Bitterness is the fruit of frustration, when one side or the other comes to believe that there is not only no understanding on the other side, but no attempt to understand. Alan Fox writes with great wisdom: 'A management which fully accepts the reality of work-group interests, which conflict quite legitimately with their own, will seek honestly and patiently to understand the cause of particular group practices in the full awareness that imaginative understanding is a pre-condition of success in modifying behaviour.'[30]

In the key posts of the union are the shop stewards. Their first loyalty is to the union. The union makes use of them, makes them feel that they are important for their fellow workers and for the union itself. They find themselves (as I have reported a shop steward's wife as saying) 'always on the telephone'. They know that they matter, they count. Down town is their full-time officer, probably a former shop steward himself, genuinely anxious to support and help shop stewards, perhaps with a 'surgery' open to them every Saturday morning. Of course, the self-respecting worker likes to feel that in some sense he is able to stand on his own feet, protect his own interests, maintain his own rights, and perhaps help to gain better conditions for his mates. In all this, the union is his ally, openly or behind the scenes. L. R. Sayles and George Strauss write: 'In our society, many employees are unhappy when they are completely dependent on someone else for the satisfaction of their needs. Even when that "someone else" is very good . . . workers tend to be uneasy when they have no power to control the benefits received.'[31] The union gives them a whiff, sometimes a taste of power. It may not be real. It may lead only to redundancy in the end, but the worker hopes not. He grasps this hope and will not give it up. Management, with its greater security, needs to try to understand what these unions in the midst of industry signify to the worker. When management begins to understand, management will begin to react constructively. What seems to be provocation becomes understandable. Management sometimes seems unaware of the dread of redundancy. Once management realizes that this above all else is what troubles the worker, inevitably management's attitude and aims are affected. The situation is becoming humanized.

Management knows and likes the senior shop steward, John, of chapter 5. Management has sent him to the USSR to see the Togliatti works there. John is keen for the success of the firm for which he works; he is cheerful and hopeful and co-operative. But he would never accept a promotion which would separate him from his union. He has said so to me. Good management can, over the years, win workers' loyalty. At BL Oxford, union leaders speak, sometimes with emphasis, of 'dedication', of genuine keenness for the company's success. It is a shame if management cannot see that loyalty to a company can indeed be generated, so long as the worker is not expected to forsake his loyalty to the union. Management has to see that undivided loyalty to the company cannot be asked of John. He cannot become 'totally involved' in the company. Much of his time and mental energy will always be given to union affairs. Yet his capacity for involvement with the company remains enormous. It ought to be fully used.

Before the end of this long chapter, two points need to be

reiterated. The first is that the loyalty to the union which needs to be freely accepted by management as a fact of real life is to the union where it really is and where its basic power lies, on the shop floor. The second is that when social realists speak of participation, it is of participation not according to a pattern but according to need and capacity. Need and capacity vary considerably.

The general public does not understand the first point. The public thinks of the unions primarily in terms of national figures who appear on television screens. The public does not understand the union base on the shop floor. Yet people can read in their papers of groups of trade unionists which choose to reject the advice of shop stewards and senior shop stewards and national executives. Mr Terry Duffy, President of the AUEW, made his union's position plain on 6 February 1980. With reference to the strike at the BL Longbridge (Birmingham) plant proposed by the National Executive of the AUEW in support of the dismissed convener, Derek Robinson, Mr Duffy said: 'We can't compel people to take strike action if they don't want to.' This was not reported in *The Guardian* of 7 February. It ought to have been shouted from the house-tops. It was in fact acted on by the local AUEW West Birmingham District Committee. In the meantime, the committee was to meet with the 300 AUEW shop stewards at Longbridge, and then to meet again to make a decision. It was eventually decided to remit the decision to a mass meeting of the Longbridge workers to be held on 20 February. Mr Bill Jordan, the AUEW district organizer, declared that he felt this to be the most democratic way of considering the dispute. At the mass meeting on 20 February, it was decided by a show of hands estimated on television to consist of 11,000 against 1000 that the union's recommendation to strike be rejected. *The Guardian* (twice) said that there were 15,000 against the strike. 'Almost 15,000 arms shot into the morning sky. . . ,' it wrote, 'and the man they dubbed Red Robbo was condemned to the dole queue.'[32]

Not always, but more and more frequently, power can be perceived to lie where the workers are. This gives to wise management considerable opportunity. In February 1979, for example, BL senior shop stewards recommended a strike to the BL work force, because of management's alleged failure to fulfil an agreement on wage rises. The union members by a two-to-one majority rejected the call to strike. Again, the unofficial BL United Craft

Organization called for indefinite strike action on behalf of craftsmen's wage rates, to begin on 6 April 1979. One hundred and fifty shop stewards from fifteen of the thirty-four BL car plants were alleged to support the appeal. When Mr Roy Fraser, the leader of the United Craft Organization, was told in a Radio Oxford interview that his union seemed to be against him, his reply was: 'I define the union as the membership on the shop floor.' He was right. On the day before the proposed strike, Radio Oxford reported that senior management was 'prominent on the shop floor' at Cowley. It was on the shop floor that the battle against the proposed strike was won. On the shop floor ultimate union power in the factory lies. This fact of industrial life is of great significance. Employers, managers, shop stewards need to face up to the opportunity which it gives for industrial leadership. Not all employers would agree with the anti-collectivist economics (and politics) of the distinguished veteran Austrian economist, Professor F. A. Hayek. Yet there is truth in what he says when he declares that: 'Not individual but group selfishness is the chief threat.'[33] To the extent that this generalization is true, authority would be wise to remember that it has a real chance of influencing individuals, and (through individuals) of influencing the union on the shop floor. If it does not come much into contact with individuals, what hope is there?

When the Confederation of Engineering and Shipbuilding Unions, consisting of seventeen unions dominated by the AUEW, had ordered a weekly strike to continue on Mondays in support of a wage claim for a minimum of £80 and with a reduction of the working week, the BBC reported that there was a shop-floor revolt in the Midlands at the end of August 1979. It declared that 'Assembly workers at Cowley have persuaded their shop stewards to let them work on Monday in opposition to the engineering unions' call for further Monday strikes.' *The Guardian* of 1 September commented that 'the Leyland revolt makes sense'. It reported Mr Bobby Fryer, a senior shop steward, as saying that 'shop stewards had done their best to carry out the unions' instructions, but they had to take their members' views into account'. The *Oxford Mail* reported on 3 September that Oxford men had defied the unions and that most of the 17,500 manual workers at six car plants in the Oxford area had ignored the call to join a national strike. All this illustrates local power, and local power provides a challenge to wise management.

It is interesting to read an account by the Labour Editor of *The*

Times of an incident in the 1978–79 suspension of the publication of the paper. He writes that the Chairman of Times Newspapers Ltd, as a result of a meeting with the unofficial 'All-Union Liaison Committee', 'conceded that power had shifted to the chapels'.[34] Consequently, Sir Denis Hamilton formally announced management's conversion from the 'mistaken policy of dealing first with trade union leadership'. This surely is most significant.

In so far as it is true that trade union power does lie on the shop floor, there is no inconsistency with the principle clearly stated in the last edition of the *TGWU Members' Handbook*: 'The first unit of organization is the branch, which is of first-rate importance, being, in fact, the foundation upon which the Union is built.' It goes on: 'The branch is the general meeting-place of the members, who, after all, ARE the Union.' Branch meetings may be ill-attended; but the members of the union have unique authority over their own work, to give it or to withhold it. Despite the limitations of the educational system, they are becoming increasingly rational people. They are capable of thinking for themselves. A rational approach to them, not to say a friendly approach (rather than a threatening one), might well have considerable effect. Relationships have in these days to be existential, as parties feel their way towards understanding with others, with others whose rationality has been quickened, making them all the more interesting to deal with.

At the CBI National Conference of 1978 a Scottish industrialist pleaded with great emphasis: 'Companies and industries are clearly not all at the same starting gate in the participation stakes, and I see it as an imperative that all be encouraged to give high priority to the working up and implementing of participation procedures which are most appropriate to their company or their industry.' Step by step, by consultation and by growing participation, involvement needs to develop towards productivity and profitableness, towards justice for all parties and the building of community. The 'involvement' of the unionists may not be total; but it may still be very worthwhile for all.

To illustrate the important fact that participation must grow only according to existential need, let me tell a sad little tale from recent personal experience. In a factory celebrated for its theory of management and for its genuine care for its workers, one dinner-hour I found myself alone for a few minutes with the four leading trade unionists. It was between a series of morning meetings (with lunch in the single-status dining-room) and an afternoon consultative meeting. Very quietly and a little sadly the union men (and a woman) closed around me. They asked what they were to call me. I told them to use my Christian name. One after another, each made his point. Without bitterness but with an obvious sense of disappointment and frustration, they quietly told their story: 'Nothing comes out of the schemes'; 'the meetings lead to nothing'; 'ideas don't materialize'; 'the system suits the management, it doesn't suit the work force'; 'it's a failure because it's had too much publicity'; 'the only real benefit is that it's given us a close relationship with management'. We moved on to the afternoon meeting; I was rubbing my eyes. Relationships were good, aims were high, but there was a lack of realism about the application of theory. There is no correct philosophy and no blue print for participation. Men's capacity for participation is conditioned by their background, their tradition, the history of the industries and plants in which they work, the experience of different unions. Justice demands that men be carefully studied, that human beings be treated according to human need.

9 Trust Relationships

A case has been presented for the acceptance of a wide measure of participation, including participation of trade union representatives in management where justice towards men of ability demands it, and where involvement and productivity will follow. This would mean changes of structure where circumstances required them. These would he hard, but not impossible, for management of the old school to accept. Right developments of structure need to be clothed in humanity, if industrial relations between human beings are to become good, and if the just community within industrial enterprise is to be created. *The Guardian*, in discussing industrial relations in Britain on 21 January 1980, made a terrible judgment on 'our older industries'. It declared that, amongst a 'complex of causes' of our present industrial ills, there is 'a common thread . . . a lack of mutual identification with the future of the firm by workers and management'.[1] This is to distribute blame and to challenge both sides of industry.

In this chapter we are searching within the realities of industry in Britain for possibilities of justice towards one another on the part of the two sides of industry. It is arguable (although by no means proven) that there was in medieval times an order in which men were taught to treat one another justly. By the end of the nineteenth century few traces of whatever good there had been in the medieval order remained. D. H. Lawrence, writing *Women in Love* in 1913, with personal knowledge of the Nottinghamshire coal field, described the change of atmosphere in a mine when the old mine-owner gave way to his son. The old man was rich, but he was kind to any man or family in need. The miners recognized his genuine care for them and touched their caps in friendly respect as they received their weekly pay. The young man changed all that. 'He knew the colliers said they hated him. . . . When they streamed past him at evening, their heavy boots slurring the pavement wearily, their shoulders slightly distorted, they took no notice of him, they gave him no greeting whatsoever, they passed in a grey-black stream of unemotional acceptance. They were not important to him, save as instruments, nor he to them, save as a supreme instrument of control.' Lawrence wrote of the mine as the young man transformed it: 'The working of the pits thoroughly changed, all the control was taken out of the hands of the miners. . . Everything was run on the most accurate and delicate scientific method, educated and expert men were in control everywhere, the miners were reduced to mere mechanical instruments.'[2]

The difference between the old man and the new was that the miners trusted the old man after a sort. Despite his dedication to capitalism and the faults (as it seemed to some of them) of that system, the men believed that he cared, that he was not only their employer but their friend. It was not a perfect relationship, perhaps not a just one, but at least there was the seed of trust there. The miners came to him in their hour of need; he listened to them, accepted their word and was generous to them. To some extent at least mine-owner and men believed in one another, counted upon one another, tried not to let one another down.

Lack of trust is a sore in the flesh of British industry. In many places it will remain divided and therefore handicapped until trust has been generated. It was tragic to hear a responsible (and Christian) senior shop steward say to me of management that it 'had better keep off the shop floor' because he did not trust it. It is devastating to hear of a good electrician, a shop steward, willing to work with management but frustrated by his experience of trying and failing to do so. 'To be honest,' he said to me, 'I do not trust the management. . . They are managing by fear. That is not the sign of good management. . . Every time there's the slightest hiccup they come to us and say "Your job will not be here." ' He added: 'Together we could get around the table and solve the problem. If you could get that sort of rapport, your problems would be few.' He went on: 'They ask for trust, but they don't foster it.' It was a cry from the heart. Much later in the year, he gave up and went to work for a smaller firm, where relationships could be established.

Modern management, good management, is inevitably busy. Desk work and committee work is unlimited (except for the very wise, who understand how to delegate to others). One Managing Director said to me that he ought to have a bed in his office, because of the time he had to spend there at night. Management is tempted to shut itself up in its offices, faithfully protected from people (who take up precious time). Geographical and physical factors make the visibility and the accessibility of top management difficult to arrange. The late Director of the CBI made a challenge and an appeal to his colleagues in management: 'And I say to you, all of you, at whatever level of the firm . . . get out from behind your desks, stop pussy-footing around.' He told the CBI National Conference in 1979 that management means working harder to create the right conditions ('a true single status society'), making better use of resources so that everyone can work efficiently, above all treating all members of the work force as human beings. Sir John asked for high profits for industry, high salaries for management, and hard work to qualify for and ensure them. That is not an altogether unreasonable demand. Even severe critics of management, even union leaders, are not bent on wrecking; rather, they frequently want to encourage good management, productivity, profitability, international competitiveness. Behind Sir John's appeal in his CBI National Conference speech lay his knowledge that multi-plant companies tend to make top management remote. What he needed to say is that, at the cost of personal dedication and self-sacrifice, or else at the cost of devolution of authority, determining management has to be made more close. Workers must know something of the people who make the decisions which affect their lives. Only this way comes trust.

When Lord Mountbatten commanded his multi-national forces in south-east Asia, he was anxious for every member of those forces to feel personally involved in the winning of the war in that area. Consequently, he made it his business to be seen at close hand by all under his command in Ceylon, Burma, India; in this he succeeded, at the cost of flying many thousands of miles. In the course of visits to soldiers, sailors and airmen, he was able to speak not only to assembled units but to a great many individuals. He stopped in front of me, asked my opinion about a triviality, and then passed on his way, leaving me glowing, a man whose opinion had been sought by the Supremo. It was a childish feeling, but a human one.

In the pre-recorded 'obituary programme' heard after his death, he observed to Ludovic Kennedy: 'If you want to be a leader of a large number of men, you have to be known to them.' Mark

Arnold-Foster wrote of him in *The Guardian* that soldiers who had felt themselves forgotten suddenly found themselves remembered.[3] The methods of leadership which Lord Mountbatten found rewarding in south-east Asia militarily he later found rewarding politically when he became Viceroy of India. It is obvious that these methods of leadership are not irrelevant to leadership in industry.

Roy Roberts, at present Managing Director of Guest Keen and Nettlefolds, said to me that 'in a badly run plant the fellow at the top is inaccessible'. He was good enough to allow me to record the conversation during a meal. I hear the chink of glasses at the same time as I hear him saying that 'general management, supermanagement, must be able to cross the shop floor, note how it is greeted, feel the atmosphere'. That is part of the job, he told me. He went on to say that it is not enough for management to be good either with policy or with men. Management must be good with both.

There is a real danger that 'personnel', a type of management created to minister to human needs, may become an obstacle to the development of trust relationships in industry between management as a whole and the work force. There is sometimes a feeling that personnel belongs to management and yet is not management itself. A young artisan gave me his impression of a personnel manager: 'He really runs the place. He's the only one we call Mister.' There was resentment, a sense that there had been usurpation of authority. Wisdom and experience combine to demand that all management accept responsibility for personnel. In British Oxygen, the Operations Director stressed to me that he and the Industrial Relations Director work closely together. Kevin Hawkins writes that 'in many companies the responsibility for industrial relations still rests with line management'.[4] David Waller, Second Brewer at Greene King (Westgate) Brewery in Bury St Edmunds, is emphatic. There is an employee relations adviser at the brewery, but there is no personnel director or manager or department. 'We claim to be personnel men,' says Mr Waller, speaking of management. There is no evading of responsibility for personnel amongst the chemists and biochemists at the brewery.

There is a price to be paid for all this. Geoffrey Wilson, of the Delta Group, says that industrial relationships are time-consuming for management. He agrees that as Joint Managing Director, he needs expert help, but he adds that he cannot delegate ultimate responsibility. He speaks from experience of good relationships. On the other hand, a Midlands mechanical engineer complains that he cannot talk with authority to his men about conditions of work because that is the prerogative of 'personnel'. In a Lancashire plant a non-militant but perceptive and honest young electrician says that personnel makes a mess both of his credit transfer and of his right to have a replacement for his industrial boots; he says that it does not seem to care for those workers' interests which the company specifically delegates to it. If a worker goes to personnel with a problem, he says that he is fobbed off. In fact, the Lancashire plant referred to has ceased to exist, the workers all made redundant. Our electrician has obtained a good job in a smaller plant. He is a happier man.

Management does sometimes seem to recruit oddly for personnel. When this happens, not only do the workers' interests suffer, but the position of management as a whole in the minds of the workers is damaged. The Australian consulting industrial and occupational psychologist, Gavin Sinclair, speaks slightingly of personnel men as he has known them in his country: 'In most large employing organizations, the personnel manager, and most of his staff, are held in low regard, if not contempt, by employees.' He believes that a personnel manager is in fact the mere stooge of senior management. 'He has been put there because of top management's belief that a loud "good bloke" will con the work force into believing that the company is essentially a people-orientated institution.'[5] I must admit that I have heard English workers talking in the same way.

Sometimes the foreman or supervisor is not of great assistance in achieving trust relationships between management and workers. A good foreman can be an inspiration to the man on the line; a bad foreman can do much harm. An EETPU shop steward tells of the foreman whose usual response is: 'That's nothing to do with me.' He tells me of how, in talks concerning the re-structuring of the department, the shop stewards gave the maintenance manager their full co-operation. He himself suggested the inclusion of the senior foreman in the talks. The foreman came. He had nothing to say, nothing to contribute. 'For all he said he might as well have been a cardboard cut-out.' On another occasion the foreman was still making out work programmes for the following week for men who by that time would no longer be working in his department. He knew this perfectly well, but he had not been officially notified. That was their problem, he said, stupidly. The authors of *Shop Stewards in Action* quote workers on the subject of foremen: 'The trouble is there is too much dishonesty. Nobody believes what anybody else says. If the foreman says it's raining, the steward won't believe him and has to look outside to check for himself.'[6]

A middle-aged, responsible worker at Cowley declares that there are too many foremen (one foreman to twenty men, he said in November 1978). He thinks that senior foremen ought to be cut out, and that only a superintendent and his team of foremen are needed. He says that foremen are standing around with folded arms doing nothing. 'There's no need for them all,' he repeated. 'The company ought not to be paying the likes of them.'

In his evidence to the Donovan Commission, Alan Flanders commented that line management takes too limited a view of its responsibilities.[7] If foremen are to play their part in industry it must be one which encourages confidence in them and which gives them confidence in themselves. Mr D. H. Markes, from his experience in management, says that foremen are the men on whom business structure is built, as the British Army is built on the non-commissioned officer. He admits to me that foremen are sometimes wrongly chosen and lack leadership quality. Yet he claims that they can provide motivation which is greatly needed. An industrial correspondent of *The Guardian* commented on the 1978 strikes of foremen and supervisors at Ford's of Dagenham. More than 2000 of these, he says, were employed for 25,000 hourly-paid workers. He noted that during their absence on strike the line moved on. He went on to comment, however, on the important role of the foreman in building up a good working relationship with his men. 'Under the noisy, relentless pressure of the assembly line, tempers are easily frayed,' he said. He added that most foremen were respected, as they went about their jobs.[8] It was an unsolicited testimonial at an unpropitious time.

There are training courses available for foremen. Yet it is not only external training courses that foremen require. Internal help is also needed, encouragement from discerning management which realizes the potentiality of the foreman or supervisor for industrial relations. Some managers claim to recognize foremen as part of the management team, yet they treat them with little respect and give them scant confidence. An awful example from Australia may bear little reference to conditions in British industry: 'A newly promoted foreman, in one of Australia's largest mining companies, persuaded his new crew to make an all-out attempt, during the very first shift he supervised, on the shift production record. They broke the record. The only acknowledgement he (or they) received was a verbal rebuke from the superintendent, for having neglected his paper work.'[9]

The (frequently) young supervisor of today looks different from the traditional picture of the foreman. In his dress, his hair-style, his speech, he is indistinguishable from the shop steward. He may have been a shop steward himself. Young management tends to promote young men on the grounds of capacity and potentiality rather than for reasons of seniority. The young man when promoted must have sufficient wits to deal with tact and patience with the older men who have been passed over. ('Let them say, if they wish: "Of course, I was offered the job, but I turned it down," ' says Steve.) The foreman may well belong to the foremen's branch of the union. Many foremen continue to vote Labour as they have always done. Steve believes in socialism and is chairman of his local Labour Party in Ebbw Vale. John is shop steward for the foremen's branch of his union. John agrees that it is the job of the foreman to 'provide motivation' for the workers. He and Steve get on well with the shop stewards, they say; they and the stewards understand and like one another. John meets his workers outside working hours at a café which he and his wife run. Some of the young foremen are open-minded, seeking for new insights, with a capacity and a will to learn. Also they are keen for further promotion. Yet some of them are dismayed by management as they meet it. 'Too many are in their offices, or going places, or showing people round,' one foreman says. 'There are not enough of them on the shop floor.'

Foremen, like all management, need to be trained. 'Without well-trained foremen and supervisors,' says Douglas Markes, 'management will be a failure.' Courses in Supervisory Studies are available at some Colleges of Further Education, and the ASTMS runs residential courses for supervisors at its college at Bishop's Stortford. The Industrial Society has courses for 'supervisors as leaders', for 'basic supervision', for 'experienced supervisors', and (most interestingly) joint courses for 'supervisors and shop stewards'. In the Midlands, various Employers' Associations, Management Training Centres, Tack Training Limited, are amongst those who provide training for 'superintendents, foremen, first-line managers or those about to be promoted to these positions'. In the *Effective Supervision* courses of Tack

Training (at £95 + VAT for three days), there are sessions on leadership, on human relations and on people at work.

Yet many foremen and supervisors remain untrained. They may be chosen for courses by their companies but may not wish to go on them. 'You learn by experience,' they say. What can some bright young tutor teach them that they have not already learned? If the middle-aged (or even slightly elderly) men get to the training course, they may have difficulty in conceptual thinking and expression. What is the tutor getting at? He is trying to draw the fruits of experience out of the men on the course by questioning them. The young men, who see at once what he is getting at, rush in to supply the answers. There seems to be on these courses a lack of teaching on the mental make-up of man, on 'what makes him tick'. In the end, there is a mass of good ideas drawn out by the tutor, mostly from the young men, which the tutor endeavours to sort and arrange so that priorities are apparent. In the minds of many, especially of the older ones, there is confusion, a lack of realization of what matters most. Some of them will reject all the ideas, as having come seemingly from young men who know nothing anyway. Some will go back to their jobs, proud of having learned nothing, since they had nothing to learn. They were perhaps over-confident in themselves, or perhaps they were lacking in confidence, and afraid to own up and open up. Worst of all is that cynicism which means that they cannot be bothered. So they return to work as before, as if they had never been.

Amongst workers in modern industry the strain of work on the assembly line sometimes tends to cause tension and irritability. This calls for understanding and sensitivity if industrial relations are not to turn sour. An industrial chaplain, Mike West, temporarily gave up his job to become an hourly-paid worker on an assembly line at Vauxhall Motors, Luton. He wrote afterwards:

In the early days, and when things did not go quite right, I was working flat out all day with scarcely a moment to stop to light a cigarette or to go to the toilet. On other days, by working fast for an hour or so, there was enough time to sit down for a few minutes. I have worked in other factories but I have never worked so hard as I did on those bad days. . . This relentless pressure shapes the social relations in the department. Most of the jobs were performed by one person alone, and there was little of the group cohesion created by working together on a task. Even when someone found their job very hard or even nearly impossible as I did on several days, the others have little time to help out. I found this frustrating, seeing another worker struggling with a problem but having hardly any time or energy to go to their aid. For myself, only the knowledge that no one would, or could, come to my rescue, created sufficient will to work at the speed and accuracy to keep pace with the ever-moving track. . . For several days I had to use an inferior rivet gun, whilst the correct one was repaired. This lengthened each job by only about 20 seconds, but at seven vehicles per hour that added 18 minutes to the working day, transforming a tolerable task to a near impossible one. Other relatively small extra problems arising from variations in task, equipment or materials had the same effect. This can be summarised in an abstract way by stating that for the fixed production volume a small increase in output, i.e. overcoming difficulties, requires a large increase in effort. . . Amongst my fellow workers, there was no disagreement about the need to try to limit managerial freedom over volume and speed. The difference between the Union Activists and the rest was that the former thought that by concerted action we could achieve some control over our situation whilst the latter were resigned to putting up with our position. In the two minor disputes I experienced, the debate was not so much about the actual facts of the situation, but whether we could win or whether we could afford to lose. The good personal relations between our foremen and Department Manager and the workers in the Department had little or no effect on this debate about our effectiveness in the industrial war between 'them and us'.[10]

It is all too easy for a person used to professional work to denigrate work on an assembly line. Yet Simon Fraser, with long experience of industry (and as secretary of the Liverpool Trades Council), assured me emphatically that a job on a conveyor belt could become satisfying to many a worker. He said that it does make a real difference to him, if he is clearly shown the end product and if it is explained to him just how his part in the creative process fits into the whole. Simon spoke as a worker and from experience, and I have heard a prominent Oxford senior shop steward speak similarly. Nevertheless, it is true that the work is tiring even if the line moves slowly. There may be (quite rightly) endless cups of tea from the machine nearby; there may be patience, crosswords or games of chess with oneself. The work does not suffer from what relieves monotony. Yet the worker may still go home tired, drop into a chair and sleep and sleep. Before he went home, he may have become an awkward fellow, no joy to his foreman. When he is tired, he needs patience and tolerance. This is the justice due to him.

Management, including leaders of the CBI, frequently refers to the 'too great' power of the trade unions. Sometimes employers too speak with a haughty sense of power that achieves nothing except distrust and anger. 'Once BL has made a decision, there is no going back,' said a company spokesman on 20 November 1979. Yet there may have to be a going back in the end. On the other hand, trade unions and trade unionists, both by official strikes and by wildcat strikes, sometimes resort to an attempt to coerce, rather than continue the bargaining process. This seems to be especially regrettable when it is in breach of agreements which have been freely made. Wildcat action is often due to a sense of outrage and desperation on the part of the worker. 'It's the only weapon we have,' said a skilled worker of the Unofficial Craftsmen's Organization in Oxford Town Hall on 19 April 1979. The strike at British Leyland, Speke No. 2 Plant, from 7 November until 27 February 1978, became in due course an official strike. It received much publicity, and the general impression was that it was caused by 'difficult' Merseyside workers. It was not made known to the general public that the strikers believed with passionate intensity that management had broken an agreement. This agreement concerning 'manning' was freely made in May 1972 and was called the Protected Earning Plan. The Joint Shop Stewards' Committee held that, by imposing new man assignments and track speeds without the stewards' agreement, management had broken clauses 4.3.5., 4.3.6., 4.3.7., and 4.3.8. The whole Plan had been declared to be 'binding in honour', but 'not intended to constitute a legally enforceable agreement'. Management denied breach of the agreement, but the workers had no doubt of it. If good will had been there, a reasonable joint interpretation of a straightforward agreement might have been reached. There was no good will. Later in the year 1978, after the employees had returned to work, Speke No. 2 Plant was closed. A sad episode had ended in tragedy. The workers believed that management sought reasons for closing Speke. Management denied at the time of the 1977–78 strike that this was so, but was not believed by its workers. This was industrial relations at their worst; no trust anywhere and no one believing anyone else.

It is assumed in industrial relations that there will be bluffing, sparring for position, unreasonable demands, unreasonable offers. A SLADE official told me how laughter sometimes follows in private the public presentation of a pay demand not in the least likely to be granted. This is mock warfare, one way of negotiating. Sir Derek Ezra, of the National Coal Board, faced with a claim from the mineworkers for a 40% wage rise in 1978, was only able at first to offer 3½%. Mr Joe Gormley, President of the National Union of Mineworkers, stated at the same time that his union's claim was only 'a starting point'. With Government help, the gap was eliminated. Agreement was reached, which was endorsed by a ballot of the miners. In 1979 the process began again, when the miners at their conference unanimously asked for more than they expected to get. Mr Gormley went on to explain the method. 'Negotiation,' he said, 'is the spirit of compromise.' The process takes time. In the end, it took a miners' ballot to reject the National Executive's recommendation and to accept the Coal Board's 'final offer'. The customary bluffing process of negotiation is scarcely one to encourage trust. Each side tries to deceive; there is an intention to deceive, a hope that the deceit will work.

Mr Bob Scholey, on behalf of the National Steel Corporation, declared on 11 February 1980, after a breakdown of negotiations for ending the steel strike, that if the unions had stayed to negotiate, the extra 1% would have been available'. According to the rules of the game, he could not have said so at an earlier hour. Evidently the union representatives had not understood the rules of the game. Sir Michael Edwardes made a plea to the BL Car unions on 20 February 1980 asking them not to say 'I thought they were bluffing.' Perhaps the bluffing game ought to end at a time when no one seems sure whether or not the game is being played according to the rules.

Anyhow, the game is not in fact great sport. 'Remember,' said one SLADE man to another in the course of the bargaining process, 'the other side is the enemy.' Hate had, as it were, to be stimulated. This is hard language; it need not be taken too seriously, yet it is scarcely language that helps to encourage fellowship, to build community. The union conveners at Chloride in 1977 declared: 'Always remember management gives you nothing, everything has to be fought for.' They go on: *'If it's worth having it's worth fighting for.'* Derrick George, the convener, confirms that 'management has never given a thing'. Derrick is a fine sincere man, yet management at Chloride has a good name and management strongly denies Derrick's statement. What does one make of it? We are in a low trust area. I myself heard Colin Barnett, Divisional Officer of the National Union of Public Employees (NUPE), say at a dinner in Oxford on 12 April 1980: 'Nothing has ever been offered me as a worker without pressure from a trade union.' If this was intended as a generalization, some of the instances in chapter 4 would refute it. Yet good employers would do well to ask themselves how sayings of this kind come to be made by men who are respected. A not unreasonable conclusion would be that all too often management tends to wait before doing anything for what it knows will be the inevitable demand from the unions. The answer to Derrick George and Colin Barnett (and to Chloride) is that relations should develop along the lines of regular and frequent consultation, in the midst of which problems will come up and be sorted out quite naturally without the confrontation which often arises in annual negotiations and other more formal and less frequent bargaining.

If some of these problems belong particularly to large-scale industry, hundreds of managers and unionists in smaller firms where good relations prevail might well say: 'Look at us. Small is beautiful. Devolve authority, break up into small units, where determining authority is close to the workers. Sort out the details of working life close to the place where it is lived.' In large firms, if devolved authority cannot be absolute, at least a relationship can be created in which what is done by higher authority can be quickly and competently explained. The Midlands engineering works already mentioned in chapter 4 is the subsidiary of a large group. The new young Managing Director of the works comes in with good education, experience in the Royal Navy and in industry itself, keen to be successful, anxious to master his new job. He means to learn about both the machinery and the men on the shop floor. He and his fellow managers (the Sales Manager, the Finance Manager and the Works Manager) meet fortnightly officially; unofficially they meet daily. They sometimes lunch out together at a country pub. They talk 'shop' all the time. They know all in the works, and are known. They themselves clock in each morning like their workers. The Managing Director says to me concerning 'consultation': 'We don't have formal meetings any more. We just have a close relationship.' I have known him over the years in good days and bad and I know he is honest and realistic. Of course, relationships are time-consuming. He is keen, ambitious, and works like a tiger. He says that in his works there is a 'continuous informal communication channel'. He prepares a monthly report for the group to which his company belongs, and a monthly report for his work force. The two reports say the same, but are differently worded. He says of his workers: 'They're as well aware as I am of what makes the company tick.' He says that he fires an opening shot for the annual negotiations in April, and they conclude in July.

He seems to have established between management and workers what Roy Roberts, of Guest, Keen and Nettlefolds calls an 'affinity'. When 'affinity' comes, there is understanding about the other man. There is respect for what he is, sensitivity for what he feels. When this happens, the way in which he ought to be treated becomes clear. Justice becomes possible when one understands. A human being treats a child differently from the way in which he treats an adult. In both cases he may be acting justly, but the actions will be different. The nineteenth-century Queenslander tended to treat the aborigine unjustly, because he did not recognize the full humanity of the wild aborigine. This is not to excuse the Queenslander's inhumanity, but to explain him. When one is tired or under stress, one may forget the human dignity of one's fellow human. One may also forget his human limitations. In such circumstances, the status of the other person's humanity may be at risk. Sir Keith Joseph, the Industry Minister, commented on 19 January 1980 on his meeting with the leaders of the striking steel workers: 'They spoke forcefully, but in a civilized manner.' It really ought to be considered likely by a Minister of the Crown that trade unionists who are his fellow humans will speak to him in a civilized manner.

The battlefields of industrial relations are littered with the casualties of insensitivity and misunderstanding. Judgments are pronounced in public and duly relayed in the press and on television, sometimes followed by loud threats. Almost everything is done to drive those who think themselves unjustly judged and publicly threatened into violent and irrational reaction. Mr Ray Horrocks, Managing Director of Austin Morris, declares (according to *The Guardian*) that 'we will not tolerate people who are trying to sabotage the company and its plans'.[11] In fact he may be obliged to tolerate just such people until better days, better understanding, more trust comes. Then they may change a little. It is difficult to conceive of any possible good to anyone or anything which such a statement could achieve. In a letter written in November 1978 pleading with the Prime Minister to persuade *The Times* management 'to lift the threat of suspension', the General Secretary of the National Association of Operative Printers, Graphical and Media Personnel (NATSOPA) quoted the saying that 'negotiation by ultimatum is rarely successful'.[12] He writes to me of his sincere belief that 'the essence of industrial democracy is persuasion not coercion'. Threats lead to irrationality when rationality is what is needed.

Mr Arthur Scargill, the Yorkshire miners' leader, with a reputation for communist militancy (although he is a Labour Party man), is reported on the BBC as saying that any miner who wants a strike must be mad. It may be difficult for those who do not care for his style of trade unionism to believe in his sincerity. Those who know him would vouch for it. There at least is a clue to the working of his mind (and to the working of the minds of the miners). It ought not to be lightly dismissed by those who assume that unions are always spoiling for a fight. There ought not to be a need to doubt everything which the other side says. People on both sides of industry often say what they mean. Let the habit grow. Alan Fox rightly denigrates the 'legitimizing' of bargaining, and 'its accompanying tactics of threats, falsification of positions and general gamesmanship'. He pleads for a reasonable assumption that between two sides 'at some level objectives are shared' and that 'problem-solving' is a possibility.[13]

If there is no local trust, then there will be exasperation, sometimes desperation, sometimes strike-proneness. The distinguished Roman Catholic weekly journal, *The Tablet*, writes:

> The essence of the decision to strike is the assertion of human dignity, the resistance of some inflicted diminishment. 'We are offended; we will not stand for it' is the cry of every striker, and the sense of having been offended is always real and deeply felt. It is this sense that needs to be analysed, for it pertains to the dignity of the human person. It is, itself, a claim to an absolute value. A striking social worker, train driver, lorry driver, hospital porter, fireman, or whoever, is refusing to be merely a social worker, train driver, and so on by ceasing (temporarily) to be one at all, and by becoming a human person stripped of his role in order to show to the rest of us who he really is. Someone we can no longer take for granted as a two-legged machine. Someone who can hurt us. It is for our con-

venience that he plays his role, as it is for his that we play ours. We take it for granted that he will, but we have no right to. And the more we abuse and deride a man who strikes, the more reason he has to defend his right to do so. The assertion of one's own human dignity and value is a claim towards transcendence, a move in the direction of God: the pity of it is that our industrialized, mechanized and centralized society depends upon a general willingness by most people most of the time to be mere cogs in the wheel, diminished and ignored.[14]

George Flint, formerly a British Motor Corporation shop steward, speaks on Radio Oxford of the worker's 'lashing out' in 'helpless frustration'. He declares that strikes are 'rarely about money' but are rather 'a bursting safety-valve, a crying for help from people trapped in an unhealthy situation'.

Realization of the need for trust is being forced upon us. The full evidence of this need cannot be given here. It is, however, to be found in magisterial style in Dr Alan Fox's *Beyond Contract: Work, Power and Trust Relations*. In this objective and comprehensive work, without sentiment or rhetoric, the accumulated evidence of sociological researchers is presented. It demonstrates clearly that a trust relationship is necessary for the good functioning of industry. Quoting from more than 200 modern sociologists, Alan Fox shows that there will be no good relationships within industry unless workers can trust management and management will trust the workers. He defines the 'high trust relationship' which is required as one 'in which the participants share certain ends and values; bear towards each other a diffuse sense of long-term obligations; offer each other spontaneous support without narrowly calculating the cost of anticipating any equivalent short-term reciprocation; communicate freely and honestly; are ready to repose their fortunes in each other's hands; and give each other the benefit of any doubt that may arise with respect to goodwill or motivation.'[15]

Alan Fox writes also of 'the low discretion syndrome', of 'low discretion roles'. In these, the worker sees himself as one who cannot be trusted, to be constantly supervised and inspected, tightly regulated in his actions in order to secure co-ordination with others, with little or no autonomy on the job, no scope for initiative, no sense of expertise, no challenge to his capacity. 'Low discretion work roles in the context of Western industrial societies tend to generate low-trust relations,' he concludes. He describes 'low-trust relations' as 'suspicion; jealousy; the misreading of men's motives which, when acted upon, becomes a self-fulfilling prophecy; the inhibitions to co-operation; the blockages created in the handling of differences and disagreements; the blight on fellowship and compassion; the withering of community'.

He is emphatic 'that organizational and societal stability depends upon there being limits to the incidence of low-trust relations'. He pleads for the will to look in unpromising circumstances for new approaches to the co-operation and sense of fellowship in community that industry needs if it is to get on with the job. He suggests serious consideration for a society in which there should be shared purpose, reduced suspicion, manifest effective concern with the low-paid and deprived. He asks for recognition that intrinsic satisfactions are a proper part of the compensation for work and for assurance that low-discretion roles are not intended as the means by which men are used to create and support privilege. Rather, in so far as they have to be, they should serve ends which those who fulfil them can respect. He asks for re-examination of the numerous conventions governing decision-making and rewards in work organizations in respect of their relevance and fairness. He claims that the present unsatisfactory state of industrial relations demands experiment. He himself calls for strategy, 'a conscious mobilization', a radical reconstruction which seeks to rally major sections of society behind shared purposes of social justice'. He believes that such a policy could be pursued by all sorts of men who would see it as serving economic rationality.[16]

No one who will take the trouble to read the cumulative social and economic case for high-trust relationships made in Fox's book can fail to gain food for serious thought. The case for such relations is so fully researched and so clearly and logically developed, that it stands almost above challenge. Alan Fox himself in Oxford keeps in touch with young management and young shop stewards. After the strikes of 1979 and 1980, it may be that some will be prepared to think harder and seek further in vigorous pursuit of the means of achieving better industrial relations. Let them face the fact that where there is injustice or what seems to be injustice there can be no peace in industry. Peace is the fruit of trust, and trust the fruit of justice. Justice generates trust; trust leads to better relationships; better relationships lead to better understanding of what in fact is just. Community develops. 'The task of the most advanced societies,' said the great sociologist, Emile Durk-heim, in 1893, 'is, then, a work of justice.'[17]

We must go round in circles, if need be, to make this point. Laboriously, from principle and with determination, trust has to be won through the personal contact of management and men. *The Guardian*, in a leading article concerning the thirteen-week steel strike of 1980, declared that the comments of Mr Bill Sirs, the 'moderate' General Secretary of the Iron and Steel Trades Confederation, went 'well beyond the standard trading of insults during a strike'. The article went on: 'When Mr Sirs commented a week ago, "We have no trust whatsoever in the people across the table from us," he was registering a long term crisis of confidence which, if unresolved, will poison working relationships long after the current troubles are history.'[18] These are tragic words.

With all this understanding-justice-trust relationship-community syndrome in mind, let us take a last (but not despairing) look at some of the problems of BL Cars. We have seen that there is a pay question. It concerns the incapacity of the nationalized company to pay all that the workers believe they ought to receive; and it also concerns the differentials between the pay of skilled, semi-skilled and unskilled workers. Besides all this, there is the need for BL Cars to increase productivity in order to compete with the higher productivity of car manufacturers on the Continent and in Japan. In the March 1980 Final Draft of Proposed Agree-ment, BL Cars ask their workers to agree to 'the introduction of sound working practices and elimination of restrictive demarca-tions which are not justified by the needs of the job, of restrictive practices and of all other constraints upon effective operating'. In the same document, management asks for 'the maintenance of efficient work organization and consistent work standards through the establishment of Industrial Engineering Techniques', with 'full co-operation in the movement of labour to ensure the efficient continuity of production'. It agrees that there may sometimes have to be 'domestic consultations on the detailed application of these principles'. It demands that 'where this occurs such consultations will not cause undue delay where speedy action is necessary to ensure the continuation of production'. In addition, there is to be 'the implementation of an incentive scheme which will provide bonus payments for plants which maintain and/or improve above the threshold levels of productivity'.

The Guardian, in referring to these proposals, makes a com-ment which demonstrates an understanding of the underlying problems of BL Cars. 'Some time soon,' it says, 'and the sooner the better, Leyland, having demonstrated its ability to run rings round organized labour, might well turn its mind to some regular institutionalized way of talking with its workers.'[19] This will not mean the sending out of another letter to workers or directive to management; it will not mean a series of speeches. What it will mean is a determination by top management to get over to middle management and to line management by tireless and unceasing personal endeavour and by every conceivable manner of communication the fact that those who work near to one another geographically must learn to listen and talk to one another. The sticking up of notices and the circulation of drafts of proposed agreements is not enough. What is required is the serious acceptance by those in management of the principle that every worker matters, that he must be spoken to, that he must be treated as if he counts. That is to say, there must be a recognition of the obligation to treat all workers with justice. This chapter is the climax of an appeal to both sides of industry that they should consciously aim at the doing of justice and thereby achieve a trust relationship. Such a relationship in modern industry also requires that management treat with justice such pluralist bodies within industry as the trade unions, which form an integral part of many working men's lives. If genuine trust relationships are to be created, it is also reasonable to ask those same trade unions to accept the principle of justice as one to be aimed at in their conduct towards management and employers.

Those prepared to defend management at all costs, as well as those caring with passionate conviction for the reputation of management for justice towards workers, ought at least to glance at the annual reports on health and safety in manufacturing and service industries. In the construction industry in North and East Scotland, for example, the Factory Inspectorate blame management for 68 out of 100 fatal accidents over a period of six years. 'In these cases,' says *The Guardian*, quoting from the Inspectorate's report, 'the accidents were reasonably foreseeable and action should have been taken by management before they occurred.'[20] This 1976 report of the work of HM Factory Inspectorate gives 382 as the figure for fatal accidents in industry during the year 1976. In 1977, the Health and Safety Executive recorded a total of 325,000 accidents at work, including the shocking number of 514 fatal ones. There were also 867 deaths arising from occupational disease. During the first six months of 1979 the HSE recorded 316 fatal accidents. 'Safety and health at work,' says the 1976 report, 'is a matter of efficient management.' Employers are bound in law to set out a statement of their safety and health policy. Inspectors in one area reported on declared that 'little attempt had been made by senior management to enforce the "organization and arrangements" section of the statement, and middle and junior management were lamentably unaware of their duties and responsibilities'. The report states baldly that 'factory inspectors have not been encouraged by what they have seen' of the implementation of policies of care for the safety and health of the employees. Ought not this to be described as shameful? The report referred to the apparent 'shock to the management of factories . . . that the preparation of the policy statement was not the end of the exercise but merely the beginning'. From all areas the report identified 'a complete lack of detail about the arrangements for ensuring that the policy statement was observed'. It identified 'an over-emphasis on the responsibilities of employees for their own safety'.[21]

The significance of lapses from high standards must not be exaggerated. However, the report casts doubt on the seriousness with which management sometimes takes its responsibility for health and safety. When we plead for justice from each side of industry towards the other, it is obvious that management must rightly be asked to face up seriously to what the report calls its 'ultimate responsibility' for safety. We do not live in Britain in times when irresponsibility is bearable.

Justice is not being done if avoidable risks are being taken with health or life, nor can there be trust where either is unnecessarily threatened at work. The careful, thorough, painstaking rendering of justice expressed in the maintenance of the highest possible standards of safety precautions is a foundation for and an example of the rendering of justice to one's fellows in community that breeds trust and builds up that community.

10 The Way Forward

If we are to move forward towards better industrial relations, towards real community in industry, the best way is by development of trust relationships. These, I believe, could be achieved through the sincere acceptance by all parties of the principle of justice towards one another and by the working out together of its implications. In this final chapter I try to suggest how to apply such a method for the achieving of such a goal.

However, we ought first to ask ourselves one question. Would the British industrial worker prefer not to work at all, to be permanently as it were 'on strike', provided that adequate means of subsistence be somehow found for him? Is he, through sin or physical constitution, 'naturally' lazy, work-shy? The threat (if it is a threat) of the coming industrial robot must mean more redundancies temporarily, if not permanently. Those who know the industrial workers (as opposed to those who read about them in the newspapers or who see them on television) know that men prefer work to unemployment, however well 'rewarded' that unemployment may be. What the industrial worker could well do with would be shorter hours of labour, and it is along these lines that the future ought to lie in so far as industry can afford these shorter hours. In some of these shorter hours, when they come, more work will be done. As for work itself, Gavin Sinclair, from his Australian experience, declares that people will work energetically and productively if certain conditions are fulfilled. The conditions, Mr Sinclair writes, are firstly that workers should be able to see the point, the justification for the effort, and secondly that they should receive satisfaction from making that effort, the satisfaction of doing it and having it acknowledged and rewarded. Lastly, adds Mr Sinclair, they should be able to respect their leaders.[1] All this sounds reasonable enough, except that the 'respect' which their leaders must win from them must add up to trust itself. The 'seeing of the point' and the 'receiving of satisfaction' are surely elements in involvement and of that justice to which human beings have a right. Given that justice, there is no problem over the average worker and his will to work. An Oxford workman, whom I tackled about the amount of 'overtime' he must be earning for work out of working hours, replied with casualness and sincerity: 'No, we've got to get the work done.' He went about it cheerfully, and did it well.

As we have seen in chapter 2 and elsewhere, it is not enough to be free from strikes. In some strike-free areas of industry where a nominal peace reigns, there are tensions inhibiting both fellowship and productivity. The ideal of the 'social contract' (such as it was) has long since perished, and there is a lack of inspiration amongst employers and unionists, despite fervent appeals at the CBI National Conference and despite the small groups of dedicated Trotskyists amongst trade union members. The tensions which exist rise quickly to crisis point; then industrial warfare becomes the means of measuring strength, and strength rather than right prevails. In the consultations, the bargaining and negotiations which precede industrial crisis, it is surely legitimate to ask both sides of industry to take into account the justice of the various proposals and to aim at a settlement which seems just to both sides. If the word 'justice' cannot be accepted for the tongue, at least the concept of justice may be accepted by the mind in the cause of good relationships.

I am appealing for a way out of devastating disorder. Industrial action amongst engineering workers in 1979 was to a very large extent played down by the television and the press. It did not make pictures or headlines. In fact, it left companies short of cash. Large and small companies were dangerously affected by the once (or twice) weekly stoppages of work. At the time, a highly placed mechanical engineer said to me that this sort of industrial action 'stops us dead'. At a time when British industry and the nation have serious problems enough without industrial disputes, there is a real case for consideration anew of the need for the pursuit of social justice. The phrase itself is an honourable and meaningful one. It does not belong to the Marxists. If employers claim to be unable to pay what workers demand, it may be a good joint exercise to get together to consider what in the circumstances may be a just wage. There would be principle to that, not mere expediency, not just exercise of power. In cases where it is clearly known that there are limiting circumstances, again and again workers who are treated well and who have established relationships with management have been capable of agreeing that the wage they will accept is lower than the wage they have claimed. If the principle of aiming at a just settlement is accepted, the debate will be concerned with what is seen to be just, after considering the work done, the result achieved, the need to make a profit, the need to pay management, the need to pay the workers. Beyond all this, there will be the need to satisfy human nature and build up community. At the small Worcestershire engineering works mentioned in chapter 4, a storeman remarked to me: 'It says a lot that the men work for so little.' There was there no sense of 'being trapped' in a low-pay situation; on the other hand, there was a sense of involvement. On both sides, there was a realization (and a determination) that when more could be paid, it would be demanded and it would be received.

Demands for higher pay in nationalized industries are sometimes made because of the assumption that the national purse is bottomless, the capacity to pay unlimited, the need for profitability non-existent. It is beginning to be realized, especially since the steel strike of early 1980, that these assumptions are invalid. In Parliament on 18 January 1980, Sir Keith Joseph described the strike as a 'classic example of the British disease'. There was more than the 'British disease' to the dispute. It is always wise for those in authority to be careful about what they say of others' motives. The steel workers in fact were neither work-shy nor strike-prone. It is normally only by close contact, it is only when trust has been generated, that workers will come to believe on management's word that there are limits beyond which management cannot go. That kind of trust had not been generated in British Steel management in 1979–80.

In industry employers sometimes find themselves up against a problem of communication not of their own making. They are sometimes obliged to reason with persons of great ability but with little education. Many youngsters who left school at 15 or 16 left with small training in reasoning, and with little knowledge of the working of the economy. A 1979 Government publication (*Local Authority Arrangements for the School Curriculum*) admits that potentialities of work experience have not been explored at school and that few pupils have learnt how industry creates wealth. A recent admirable publication of the Working Together Campaign is called *The Economic Facts of Life*.[2] It teaches basic industrial and commercial economics with ability, simplicity and illustrations. It is warmly commended by the General Secretary of the AUEW and by the General Secretary of the National Association of Schoolmasters/Union of Women Teachers. It is in fact suitable for trade unionists and for teenagers. But if the trade unionists had had that kind of teaching when they were at school, they would not be in need of it now. I vividly remember teaching which I received on the economics of Free Trade and Protection when I was barely thirteen.

Dr John Rae, Headmaster of Westminster School, considers that one of the great challenges to education in the 1980s will come from the comparative failure of Britain's manufacturing industry.[3] He laments the social prejudice against the practical in schools. Not only do many schools fail lamentably in teaching mathematics and the sciences, but they seem unable to train young people to be capable of sustained rational thinking and action. We cannot, therefore, expect the mass of the work force to react with full responsibility to reasoned argument, or indeed to follow fully a train of argument based upon economic facts. We have to depend upon the training and exceptional capacity of their leaders the shop stewards, and upon workers' trust in these leaders. The very men who sometimes seem to people outside industry to be sources of disruption are in fact the men upon whose future co-operation industry depends.

There are advantages to be gained for industry from the education of trade unionists in economics itself, in costing, in pricing, in international trade. There is also, almost above all, advantage in the learning by those in authority on both sides of industry of facts about the human mind and its working. Here we are up against traditional suspicion of psychology and distrust of the 'head-shrinker', the psychiatrist. So we tend to stumble on in the field of relationships, ignorant both about other people and ourselves, because of prejudice against a subject and a name. If the need for training in economics is great, the need for training in basic psychology, in the behavioural sciences, is very great. Yet the demand for it is sometimes rejected outright, sometimes ridiculed. A chief medical officer's reply to an appeal for the assistance of industrial psychologists was unhelpful. 'First of all,' said the doctor, 'there aren't any. Secondly, they're mad. Thirdly, if they were called in, they would frighten the pants off management.'

None of these statements is true. This sort of reaction is no help to human beings in need of greater understanding of one another and of the groups with which they are concerned. The result of misunderstanding of the working of a fellow human being's mind is often tragic. People who work with people need to study people, both as individuals and as members of groups. Psychology is the science of the human mind, not at all a threatening subject, not at all to be despised, very important for relationships.

For the Council for National Academic Awards BA degree in Social Science, the Polytechnic of Central London provides a course intended to give 'a broad-based intellectual foundation for a wide range of administrative careers in business and government'. Sociology/Psychology is compulsory for all first-year students. There is also an Introduction to Psychology course, in which basic psychological and socio-psychological processes are illustrated by reference to industrial/commercial situations. The Social Psychology and Industry course deals with 'the psychology of industrial conflict, frustration and aggression, socio-psychological factors in aggression, attitude conflicts and attitude change, inaction and resistance to change, negotiating behaviour'. Surely some of these subjects ought to be studied on courses for management and for shop stewardship? The sense of frustration and that of aggression are not confined to one side of industry. In the last year of the Business Studies course, 'the social-psychological perspective is developed further, focusing upon the effect of groups and cultures upon individual and interpersonal processes'. All this belongs to the three years of a university-standard course. Much of it might well be the basis of lectures and discussions amongst keen and interested men on management, supervisors' and shop stewards' courses. 'Manipulation' and 'head-shrinking' would be no serious danger to canny men on either side.

Those on both sides of industry who meet to consult or bargain will be more or less educated, more or less experienced. Their capacity for justice, their ability and willingness to recognize what is just will be uncertain, variable. These are facts which we have to face when we commend the principle of justice as a determinant to be accepted by both sides in industrial relationships. There is no suggestion that the acceptance of the principle will make good relations easy; it is rather that it will make them possible where now they seem to be impossible. In consultation and negotiation there will be times when representatives of one or both sides will be at their worst; irritability or temper will characterize their meetings. Realists who study human nature at close hand are aware of its oddity, of its eccentricity, and also of the fact that the 'difficult' man of today may be much less difficult tomorrow. Even children learn quite young that adults are erratic in their reactions, that what they say today they will not say tomorrow.

An inspector in a large West Country engineering works, a Christian, a man of balanced judgment, who has worked there for twenty-two years, cannot refrain from mentioning and regretting the 'greed' which he sees around him. With the greed, he sees also the real envy directed by some workers towards fellow workers who may be earning (or are likely to earn) more than they do. Reinhold Niebuhr writes of 'the failure of modern socially minded educators . . . to appreciate the consistency with which economic groups express themselves in terms of pure selfishness'.[4] This is a reality in life, including modern industrial life. Let us accept the existence of greed amongst workers (and amongst shareholders, employers, management). Let us accept also the existence of lust for power and other forms of selfishness which disfigure human character and damage relationships. The 'hard-facedness' of some management men is not moral, nor is the 'bloody-mindedness' of some union men. It is important that the student of industrial relations, the researcher, the consultant, should see that 'hard' face and know that 'bloody' mind. Both are for real. If he is wise in the pursuit of his task, the seeker for good relationships will try to be around when the hard face relaxes a little, and the angry mind cools down. Every day is different. Jim Hughes, Director and General Manager of Tannoy, writes to me concerning the 'Management Philosophy of Tannoy Ltd': 'As to whether our philosophy is still alive and kicking, you will probably get different answers on different days of the week.' There wisdom and experience speak. The Branch Secretary of the union at Tannoy writes to me: 'It's the build-up of small irritations which causes most withdrawals of labour.' But he adds: 'I can see that a lot of the irritations can be got rid of through group structure.' Here are men on two sides of the same industry who can have their bad days, and yet can see light, can work together. 'The benefits of this persevering working together,' writes the Tannoy union man, 'are hard for the workers to measure.' He adds that the experience has left its mark upon them. This is high praise.

In thinking and speaking of conduct and relations within industry, in facing the realities of injustice, emotional misconduct, bad temper, haughtiness, abuse, one must take care not to generalize.

It is unjust to say that 'the workers are greedy, the unions are power-hungry', that 'management is intolerant', as if these things were for ever true. On the BBC Television News at 9 p.m. on 25 January 1979, there was a report of a picket who declared that he did not see why others should not go without food because of his picketing; he himself was going without food because of his low pay. He would probably not have spoken this way the day before or the day after. He was certainly not representative of the thinking of his union colleagues. His words inevitably made an unfavourable impression on viewers. The media are neither wise nor responsible when they broadcast items of this kind. They may do considerable harm, cause serious misunderstanding. Some days some workers are greedy, some unions power-hungry, some managements intolerant. On other days, they are deflated, tired; some days they are genuinely seeking for peace, for an end to industrial selfishness. It is because men's reactions to themselves and to one another are unpredictable, that infrequent meetings must not be allowed to decide men's fate. The men's leaders are unreasonable today, management's unreasonable tomorrow. 'Negotiations,' says Mostyn Davies, a Peterborough Industrial Chaplain, 'are an area of temptation.' The day after tomorrow both parties may be rational. Even the grossly selfish have chinks in their armour. There comes the day when both parties are less than grossly selfish. That is the day.

Collective bargaining tends to have its own ethos, as it tends to have its fixed dates and time limits. *Workers' Participation in Management in Britain* is again excellent. The authors plead for a continuing blurring of the dividing line between collective bargaining and consultation. 'The ethos of a consultative committee is very different from that of a collective bargaining session,' they say. They go on: 'With consultation, management is hopeful that the discussions will be carried on in an atmosphere that is free from the threat of serious conflict if agreement is not immediately reached.'[5] Let consultation grow and become more inclusive.

Meetings between the two sides of industry ought to be frequent; they ought sometimes to be virtually free from time limits, wearing though this be. Infrequent, occasional meetings with strict time limits may have disastrous results. The tension generated, the stance 'put on' by one party or the other, may give untypical impressions of the parties, of the 'real' men. Tom meets his departmental head once a month. As we have seen, the meetings, as Tom said, are 'acrimonious'. Human beings have to learn tentatively, sensitively, over considerable periods of time, how to handle one another, not for the purpose of manipulation but for the purpose of learning to live together and work together in community. Only by a willingness to keep on meeting together, talking together, can there be an eventual meeting of minds. Then patience will be rewarded, and men can in their better moments decide on what in the circumstances is just. Then trust can be at last built up.

How does this kind of thing happen, how can justice be seen to be done, trust relationship be eventually achieved? At the Greene King Brewery, says a shop steward, negotiations for the annual pay settlement (and for any revision of the union-company Agreement which may be necessary) begin in mid-September. They must conclude by the end of October, and the new settlement comes into operation at the beginning of November. The first meeting between the unions and management has generally, says the shop steward, a 'happy family' atmosphere. At this first meeting, normally, all the shop stewards are present (from the three breweries and the three depots), with two representatives of management and two full-time officers of the TGWU. At this meeting a 'negotiating committee' is elected, with eight representatives of the union on it. There are normally five all-day meetings of the committee, held at the Greene King Training Centre, and lunch is arranged for all by the company 'somewhere in the country'. More than the five scheduled meetings can be held, if it seems that these are not going to be enough. When eventually agreement on the committee has been reached, the proposals go back for decision to the members of the union. Since 1977, there has been a ballot to decide on acceptance. The management members of the committee give the impression of being armed with discretionary powers, which render them capable of making decisions binding on management; they are in fact 'determining management'. A foreman (not himself represented on the committee) declares: 'I don't think you could do more to keep relations good.' It would be difficult to disagree with this slow-speaking, thoughtful man.

I began this study of industrial relations in Britain by giving a brief account of the course of a recent industrial conflict in Western Australia. I shall end by telling this time of the steady reduction of industrial strife in the far west of North Queensland. Here is a situation known fairly intimately to me, where through rational and just action on both sides, it seems to me that a trust relationship is in process of being built up. So let us look hard at Mount Isa Mines in north-west Queensland. Far away from large cities, with a population of 26,000 (in 1979), in a remote, drought-stricken, barren area, one of the world's large producers of lead, zinc, copper and silver employs over 5000 people. Since the disastrous strikes of 1961 and 1964–65, Mount Isa Mines has had a good record of industrial relations. There have been short isolated disputes involving sections of the work force, but it is claimed that no more than one half of 1% of working time has been lost through disputes. Here during the years since 1965, patiently, laboriously, persistently, a trust relationship seems to have grown. There has been a consensus of opinion that there should be no repetition of 1961 and 1964–65. Every two years the agreement between the company and the unions is renegotiated. In August every alternate year the unions present their 'log of claims'. The company has two months in which to consider these. During November and December the company representatives and those of the unions (including local men and permanent State officials from Brisbane) discuss the proposed new agreement. All sit around a table in a large mess hall and hammer out the details. On some days the two sides are together for fourteen or more hours. No rigid time limit is set, but there is a common recognition that agreement must be reached. Reasoned demands will normally be met by reasoned answers, and those who represent the company are 'determining managers', in the sense that they have authority to make decisions on behalf of Mount Isa Mines. All eat their midday meal together, breaks for morning tea and for coffee are sometimes called at moments of tension. Eating and drinking together (not merely in the same room) plays a part in the building of community.

It was agreed from 1966 that there would be no major variation in conditions of employment in between the two-year agreements except when there are major significant changes in community and industrial standards. However, there are also shorter quarterly meetings between the two sides, although the State officials of the union do not attend these. They provide a forum for the debating of matters of general concern, as well as for maintaining close relationships. It ought to be added that as a result of all those meetings, management and union leaders have come to know one another well. Grievance procedures have been worked out for the various unions and there seems to be a general willingness of employees with grievances to follow them. A community has developed. The work force 'stays on' much longer in 1977–78 than in 1967–68. Alex Pavusa, President of the Mount Isa Trades and Labour Council, writes: 'Having been involved from the first negotiation right through to the present, one of the most significant benefits derived from the period of the negotiations has been the tremendous development of mutual respect between the employer and employee representatives, which after all, is the very foundation of all good industrial relationships.'[6] In a strange way, people are seen and known to look after one another.

This apparent care for one another is exemplified by the emphasis throughout the mines on safety. Mount Isa Mines claim to be one of the world's largest underground mines. It also has a safety record calculated to build up trust. There is a daily safety report. Safety responsibility is bred into the staff. Sometimes miners pull up staff members in the interest of safety. Management knows its responsibility, and is constantly reminded of it. All this leads to trust.

'One cause for concern throughout Australia is the impact of technological change on the work force,' says *Mimag*, the MIM quarterly journal. 'Last December, the negotiators at Mount Isa agreed to take steps towards monitoring the effects of such changes in certain areas of work.'[7] The two sides approach the future together. Australia is not Britain. Conditions and traditions are different, yet only a very unwise person would assert that this North Queensland experiment in growing together over the negotiating table and the coffee cups has nothing to teach some industries in Great Britain.

In the achieving of a trust relationship an allegiance, explicit or implicit, to the ideal of justice is no mean asset. '*Fiat justitia ruat coelum*' (Let justice be done though the heavens fall). Not explicitly, but implicitly, in Mount Isa a sense that justice is being rendered seems over the years to have grown up. I left Mount Isa in 1962, and found different attitudes, a quite different atmosphere there in 1979. A trust relationship had developed. I was amazed. Personal contacts in mid-1980 seem to confirm this.

The theme outlined here is simple. Justice in industry will lead to trust. Hereby better industrial relations will be created. These will lead to higher productivity. All will benefit. In so far as a just industrial community can be built up, that community by its productivity will be available to minister to a more just world, in which the richer countries have an opportunity to assist more generously in the development of the poorer ones.

To what extent is all this valid? Tom, the Oxford shop steward, says that it is impossible to understand industrial relations 'from the outside'. If he is correct, what right has the church to have a word on the subject? The answer is just this: that it has indeed a right to have a word, provided that it is a listening, hearing, seeing church, seeking to speak the word of God as it sees and hears it in the midst of the sights and sounds of the world of today. It is not without representation in management and on the shop floor. Besides its excellent industrial chaplains, men of industry and of theology, the church works quietly in offices and at lathes and on conveyor belts. None of its representatives can be content with what they see and hear at present. The church is under a solemn obligation to promote the justice of the kingdom of God, in so far as it is in any measure able to do so.

'The just man justices,' wrote the poet, Gerard Manley Hopkins. The medieval Dominican theologian and mystic, Meister Eckhart, defined a just man as one who is 'conformed and transformed into justice'. If a minority of men (and women) in industry could be persuaded to be so conformed and transformed, the effect upon the majority in industry would be beyond all imagining.

NOTES

Introduction

1. *The Guardian*, 13 October 1979, p. 4.
2. Ibid., p. 24.
3. Bank of England, *Quarterly Bulletin*, September 1979.
4. *The Guardian*, 21 October 1979, p. 1.
5. *The Times*, 20 December 1979.
6. J. L. and B. Hammond, *Rise of Modern Industry*, Methuen 1925, p. 45.
7. *U.K. in Figures*, HMSO 1979.
8. *Annual Abstract of Statistics 1977*, HMSO 1977, p. 153.
9. Ibid., p. 308.
10. 'Britain's decline; its causes and consequences', *The Economist*, 2 June 1979, p. 29.
11. *The Observer*, 14 October 1979, p. 1.
12. Finniston *Report*, *Engineering Our Future*, HMSO 1980, pp. 7,12.
13. *The Guardian*, 1 December 1979, p. 10.
14. *The Guardian*, 10 December 1979, p. 12.

1 Wonderland

1. Hamersley Iron, *Iron Ore Production and Processing Agreement* (No. 28 of 1977), pp. 174–75.
2. Ibid., p. 6.
3. Letters from Hamersley Iron unions, 'Logs of claims', dated 10 May 1979.
4. Hamersley Iron, 'Notice to all employees' (undated), pp. 1,2,4.
5. Hamersley Iron, 'Notice to all employees of the company' (undated).
6. 'To all Hamersley Iron wage employees', p. 2.
7. 'Tom Price Combined Unions Committee Women's Auxiliary', 26 June 1979.
8. Reinhold Niebuhr, *Christian Realism and Political Problems*, Faber 1954, pp. 165–66.
9. Rowan Williams, *The Wound of Knowledge*, Darton, Longman & Todd 1979, p. 2.
10. The William Temple Foundation, *Bulletin 7*, October 1978, p. 1.

11. Ibid., p. 2.
12. Editorial, *Theology*, January 1980, p. 4.

2 *Misconceptions*

1. *The Australian*, 14 August 1978, p. 6.
2. Department of Employment, *Employment News*, January 1978, p. 2.
3. Department of Employment, Press release, 29 November 1978, p. 161.
4. Department of Employment, *DE Gazette*, April 1979, p. 418.
5. *UK in Figures*, 1979 edition.
6. P. K. Edwards, 'The awful truth about strife in our factories', *Industrial Relations*, Spring 1979, p. 7.
7. *DE Gazette*, November 1978, p. 1258.
8. *DE Gazette*, June 1978, p. 1.
9. *The Financial Times*, 26 April 1979, p. 20.
10. *DE Gazette*, February 1980, p. 161.
11. *The Guardian*, 31 January 1980, p. 2.
12. *The Guardian*, 25 October 1979, p. 28.
13. Letter, 5 September 1978.
14. *The Times*, 1 September 1978, p. 12.
15. Kevin Hawkins, *The Management of Industrial Relations*, Penguin 1978, p. 55.
16. Royal Commission on Trade Unions (Donovan) *Report*, HMSO 1968, p. 79.
17. Ibid., p. 77.
18. *Work Place Industrial Relations 1973*, HMSO 1975, p. 80.
19. T. Nichols and P. Armstrong, *Workers Divided*, Fontana/Collins 1976, pp. 71,72.
20. The *Spectator*, 29 July 1978, p. 3.
21. Letter to the *Spectator*, 30 July 1978.
22. Delta Metal Company, *Report*, 1977, p. 4.
23. Graham Turner in *The Daily Telegraph*, 26, 27, 30, 31 July 1979.
24. The *Church Times*, 27 October 1978, p. 7.
25. *The Guardian*, 25 August 1977, p. 7.
26. Theo Nichols and Huw Beynon, *Living with Capitalism*, Routledge & Kegan Paul 1977, p. 21.

3 *People*

1. *Living with Capitalism*, pp. 34,33.
2. Ibid., back cover.
3. Ibid., p. 35.
4. Ibid., pp. 5, 121, 4, 5, 4
5. Ibid., p. 36.
6. Eric Batstone, *British Journal of Industrial Relations*, July 1978, p. 266.

7. Richard Hyman, 'On the job', *New Society*, 25 August 1977, pp. 401–2.

8. James Mortimer, 'Negative stance', *Personnel Management*, October 1977, p. 50.

9. J. Roeber, *Social Change at Work*, Duckworth 1975, p. 194.

10. J. M. Winter and D. M. Joslin, *R. H. Tawney's Commonplace Book*, Cambridge University Press 1972, p. 35.

11. *The Guardian*, 24 January 1980, p. 10.

12. *The Sunday Mirror*, 19 March 1978, p. 4.

13. *People at Work*, Addison Wesley Press, Reading, Mass. 1977, pp. 21, 10, 4, 86, 72. Also, *Work Study*, Harrogate, January 1980, pp. 35–39.

14. M. Maccoby, *The Gamesman*, Secker & Warburg 1977, p. ix.

15. *The Supply and Control of Labour 1915 to 1916*, Volume IV, Part II, Labour Regulation and the Munitions of War (Amendment) Act, HMSO 1917–20, p. 1.

16. *R. H. Tawney's Commonplace Book*, pp. 10,13.

17. Georges Friedmann, *Industrial Society*, Free Press of Glencoe 1955, p. 13.

18. Georges Friedmann, *Problèmes Humains du Machinisme Industriel*, Gallinard, Paris 1945, p. 333.

19. *Industrial Society*, pp. 388, 374.

20. Douglas McGregor, *The Human Side of Enterprise*, McGraw-Hill 1970, p. 86.

21. Nigel Nicholson, 'The role of the shop steward: an empirical case study', *The Industrial Relations Journal*, Spring 1976, p. 20.

22. G. Sinclair, *I Only Work Here*, Holt-Saunders, Artarmon, N. S. Wales 1979, p. 136.

23. Royal Commission on Trade Unions, 1965–68, Written Evidence, [3], HMSO 1968, p. 554.

4 Management

1. John Power, letter to *The Sunday Times*, 15 January 1978, p. 14.

2. ACAS *Report No. 9*, 1977, p. 20.

3. *The Daily Telegraph*, 31 July 1979, p. 14.

4. *The Daily Telegraph*, 30 July 1979, p. 12.

5. Clarence B. Randall, *What an Executive Should Know about Management*, Dartnell Press, Chicago 1964, p. 11.

6. *The Human Side of Enterprise*, p. 23.

7. *Living with Capitalism*, p. 139.

8. Graham Turner in *The Daily Telegraph*, 27 July 1979, p. 16.

9. *The Daily Telegraph*, 31 July 1979, p. 14.

10. *The Daily Telegraph*, 26 July 1979, p. 3.

11. *The Daily Telegraph*, 27 July 1979, p. 16.

12. *The Guardian*, 7 July 1979, p. 7.

13. *The Financial Times*, 30 January 1978, p. 9.

5 The Shop Steward

1. *Work Place Industrial Relations 1972*, HMSO 1974, pp. 4–5.
2. Derek Robinson in *The Times*, 9 February 1978, p. 21.
3. Donovan Commission, *Report 17, Facilities Afforded to Shop Stewards*, HMSO 1971, p. 14.
4. Alan Fox, *Socialism and Shop Floor Power*, Fabian Society 1978, p. 9.
5. Jack Burton, *Transport of Delight*, SCM Press 1976, p. 79.
6. Donovan *Report*, pp. 26, 29, 102.
7. Ron Powell in *The Sunday Times*, 12 March 1978, p. 17.
8. G. D. H. Cole, *Introduction to Trade Unionism*, Allen & Unwin 1953, p. 46.
9. J. F. B. Goodman and T. G. Whittingham, *Shop Stewards in British Industry*, McGraw-Hill 1979, p. 23.
10. J. Hinton, *The First Shop Stewards' Movement*, Allen & Unwin 1973, pp. 79–80.
11. Ibid., pp. 23,99.
12. Donovan *Report*, p. 26.
13. *Socialism and Shop Floor Power*, p. 2.
14. Donovan *Report*, p. 26.
15. Ibid., p. 26.
16. *Facilities for Shop Stewards*, TUC, reprinted 1978, p. 8.
17. Eric Batstone, Ian Boraston and Stephen Frenkel, *Shop Stewards in Action*, Blackwell 1977, p. 202.
18. Donovan Commission, *Research Paper 10*, HMSO 1966, p. 32.
19. Huw Beynon, *Working for Ford*, EP Publishing Ltd, pp. 83, 240.
20. Bruce Partridge, 'The activities of shop stewards', *Industrial Relations Journal*, Winter 1977–78, pp. 41, 39.
21. Donovan Commission, *Research Paper 10*, p. 58.
22. *Perspective on Strikes* ed. Ronald H. Preston, SCM Press 1975, p. 72.
23. *Working for Ford*, pp. 77ff.

6 The Greeks Had a Word for It

1. Eric Jacobs, 'Open Letter to Management, *Industrial Society*, January/February 1980, p. 9.
2. *The Guardian*, 9 January 1980, p. 1.
3. *Employment and Technology*, TUC 1979, pp. 8, 9.
4. Finniston *Report*, pp. 31, 32.
5. *Parliamentary Reports (Hansard)*, Vol. 405, No. 88, columns 1362, 1364.
6. *The Guardian*, 10 February 1980, p. 1.
7. *R. H. Tawney's Commonplace Book*, p. 13.
8. Ibid., pp. 70, 72f., 55.
9. R. H. Tawney, *The Acquisitive Society*, Unwin University Books 1921, p. 222.

10. Ibid., pp. 8, 3.
11. *The Times*, 28 November 1979, p. 21.
12. *The Acquisitive Society*, p. 5.
13. F. A. Hayek, *Law, Legislation and Liberty*, Volume III, Routledge & Kegan Paul 1979, p. 128.
14. Bruno Snell, *The Discovery of the Mind*, Harper & Row, New York 1960 edition, pp. 249–250.
15. A. N. Whitehead, *Process and Reality*, Cambridge University Press 1929, p. 53.
16. Plato, *The Republic*, IV, 432; in the translation by H. D. P. Lee, Penguin Books 1955.
17. Ibid., p. 87.
18. *The Republic*, IV, 433.
19. Ibid., IV, 434.
20. *The Ethics of Aristotle* tr. J. A. K. Thomson, Penguin Books 1976, 5, 1134B.
21. D. Rees et al., *Consider Your Call*, SPCK 1978, p. 207.
22. D. K. Ross, *Rhetorica*, Clarendon Press 1924, 1422A.
23. *Ethics*, 5, 1129B.
24. John Rawls, *A Theory of Justice*, Oxford University Press 1972, pp. 3, 10, 3.
25. *The Guardian*, 30 January 1980, p. 1.
26. *Ethics*, 5, 1137A.
27. C. Bode, *The Portable Thoreau*, Penguin Books 1977, p. 111.
28. *A Theory of Justice*, p. 11.
29. Richard Hyman and Ian Brough, *Social Values and Industrial Relations*, Blackwell 1975, p. 8.
30. Kevin Hawkins, 'The future of collective bargaining', *Industrial Relations Journal*, Winter 1979/80, p. 12.
31. *Living with Capitalism*, p. 156.
32. Barbara Wootton, *Social Foundation of Wage Policy*, Unwin University Books, 1955 p. 190.
33. *The Daily Telegraph*, 15 August 1979, p. 3.
34. *The Distribution of Income and Wealth*, TUC 1976, p. 18.
35. *The Guardian*, 11 January 1980, p. 2.
36. Finniston *Report*, p. 58.
37. *Leyland Cars*, AUEW (TASS) 1977, p. 4.
38. *Engineering Craftsmen: Shortages and Related Problems*, National Economic Development Office 1977, pp. 21, 28, 29.
39. *The Management of Industrial Relations*, p. 98.
40. *I Only Work Here*, p. 67.
41. *The Guardian*, 30 November 1977, p. 13.
42. *The Guardian*, 18 August 1979, p. 15.

7 *The Christian Doctrine of Justice*

1. *R. H. Tawney's Commonplace Book*, p. 44.
2. e.g. Col. 1.27. All biblical quotations are taken from the New English Bible unless otherwise stated.
3. David Jenkins, 'Putting theology to work', *Theology*, March 1978, pp. 118–19.
4. David Jenkins, *Christian Faith and Political Hopes* ed. H. Willmer, Epworth Press 1979, p. 141.
5. B. Schlink, *A Foretaste of Heaven*, Lakeland 1975, p. 357.
6. Reinhold Niebuhr, *Christian Realism and Political Problems*, Faber 1954, p. 106.
7. *Oxford Diocesan Magazine*, November 1978, p. 14.
8. Emil Brunner, *Justice and the Social Order*, Lutterworth 1949, pp. 117–18.
9. Reinhold Niebuhr, *The Nature and Destiny of Man*, Volume II, Nisbet 1943, pp. 264–65.
10. John Bennett in *Theology and Change* ed. R. H. Preston, SCM Press 1975, pp. 138, 142.
11. *Consider Your Call*, pp. 207, 36.
12. John Bright, *Covenant and Promise*, SCM Press 1977, p. 35.
13. J. H. Cone, *God of the Oppressed*, SPCK 1975, p. 64.
14. Dr Anthony Phillips directs my attention to E. W. Nicholson, *Exodus and Sinai in History and Tradition*, Blackwell 1973, and R. E. Clements, *Prophecy and Covenant*, SCM Press 1975.
15. N. H. Snaith, *Distinctive Ideas of the Old Testament*, Epworth 1974, p. 74.
16. H. H. Rowley, *The Faith of Israel*, SCM Press 1970, p. 197.
17. W. Eichrodt, *Theology of the Old Testament*, SCM Press 1961, Vol. 1, p. 241.
18. A. Weiser, *The Psalms*, SCM Press 1962, p. 25.
19. Yehezkel Kaufmann, *The Religion of Israel*, Allen & Unwin 1961, p. 311.
20. Bernhard Anderson, *The Eighth Century Prophets*, SPCK 1979, p. 43.
21. J. Bonsirven, *Le Règne de Dieu*, Aubier, Paris 1956, pp. 7, 105.
22. Norman Perrin, *The Kingdom of God in the Teaching of Jesus*, SCM Press 1963, p. 205.
23. J. A. Baird, *The Justice of God in the Teaching of Jesus*, SCM Press 1963, pp. 205, 203.
24. *Le Règne de Dieu*, p. 105.
25. St Thomas Aquinas, *Summa Theologica*, 11, 2, Q58, A2.
26. Ibid., 11, 2, Q58, A5.
27. Ibid., 11, 2, Q58, A1.
28. Ibid., 11, 2, Q58, A12.
29. Ibid., 11, 2, Q58, A12.
30. Ibid., 11, 1Q80, A2.
31. Ibid., 11, 1Q58, A8.

32. In M. B. Reckitt (ed), *The Return of Christendom*, Allen & Unwin 1922, p. 117.

33. In F. S. Marvin (ed), *Progress and History*, Oxford University Press 1916, p. 82.

34. William Temple, *Christianity and Social Order*, Shepheard/Walwyn/SPCK 1976, p. 2.

35. Ibid., p. 37.

36. Edward Norman, *Church and Society in England 1770–1970*, Clarendon Press 1976, p. 283.

37. F. R. Barry, 'The earthly kingdom', *Times Literary Supplement*, 7 January 1977, p. 18.

38. *Christianity and Social Order*, p. 36.

39. *Consider Your Call*, p. 36.

8 Participation

1. John Wates, *Participation – The Proven Code*, Industrial Society 1979.

2. The *Church Times*, 23 February 1979, p. 1.

3. *The Management of Industrial Relations*, p. 34.

4. Ibid., p. 119.

5. *Shop Stewards in British Industry*, p. 193.

6. John Adair, *Management and Morality*, David & Charles 1974, p. 139.

7. ACAS, *Disclosure of information to trade unions for collective bargaining purposes*, HMSO 1978.

8. *Social Change at Work*, pp. 216, 194.

9. *The Management of Industrial Relations*, p. 119.

10. *Making Work More Satisfying*, HMSO 1975, pp. 9, 22.

11. *People at Work*, p. 15.

12. R. O. Clarke, D. J. Fatchett, B. C. Roberts, *Workers' Participation in Management in Britain*, Heinemann 1972, p. 5.

13. *The Management of Industrial Relations*, p. 118.

14. Finniston *Report*, p. 31.

15. Fergus Panton in *Increasing Employee Involvement*, Working Together Campaign, 1979, p. 15.

16. *The Management of Industrial Relations*, p. 126.

17. *Report of the Committee of Inquiry on Industrial Democracy*, HMSO 1977, p. 43.

18. Peter Drucker, *The New Society*, Heinemann 1950, p. 157.

19. Donovan Commission, *Research Paper 3*, HMSO 1966, p. 8.

20. 'Britain', *The Economist*, 19 April 1980, p. 49.

21. 'Science and technology', *The Economist*, 19 April 1980, p. 94.

22. *The Guardian*, 21 April 1980, p. 1.

23. *Management Today*, January 1979, pp. 41, 46.

24. *Report* from conference on 'Technology and Change in Industry', February 1980.

25. *The New Society*, pp. 81, 85.

26. M. Douglas, *Natural Symbols*, Cresset Press 1970, p. 138.

27. *The Economist*, 28 June 1979, p. 105.

28. 'The future of collective bargaining', pp. 15f.

29. Peter Berger, *A Rumour of Angels*, Penguin Books 1971.

30. *Research Paper 3*, p. 10.

31. L. R. Sayles and George Strauss, *Managing Human Resources*, Prentice-Hall 1977, pp. 77–78.

32. *The Guardian*, 21 February 1980, p. 24.

33. *Law, Legislation and Liberty*, Vol. III, p. 89.

34. P. Routledge, 'The dispute at Times Newspapers Ltd', *Industrial Relations Journal*, Winter 1979/80, p. 9.

9 Trust Relationships

1. *The Guardian*, 21 January 1980, p. 11.

2. D. H. Lawrence, *Women in Love*, Heinemann, 1954 edition, pp. 224, 223.

3. *The Guardian*, 28 August 1979, p. 15.

4. *The Management of Industrial Relations*, p. 188.

5. *I Only Work Here*, pp. 188, 39.

6. *Shop Stewards in Action*, p. 125.

7. *Written Evidence* (for Donovan Commission), HMSO 1968, pp. 554–55.

8. *The Guardian*, 8 May 1978, p. 13.

9. *I Only Work Here*, p. 36.

10. 'Three Months on the Track', *ICF Quarterly*, October 1977, pp. 10–12.

11. *The Guardian*, 24 November 1979, p. 26.

12. *The Guardian*, 28 November 1978, p. 28.

13. Alan Fox, *Beyond Contract: Work, Power and Trust Relations*, Faber 1974, p. 35.

14. *The Tablet*, 20 January 1979, p. 50.

15. *Beyond Contract: Work, Power and Trust Relations*, p. 362.

16. Ibid., pp. 25ff., 177, 317f., 353ff. et passim.

17. Emile Durkheim, *The Division of Labour in Society*, 1964 edition, Glencoe Free Press, p. 387.

18. *The Guardian*, 18 February 1980, p. 10.

19. *The Guardian*, 19 March 1980, p. 10.

20. *The Guardian*, 13 April 1978, p. 4.

21. Health and Safety *Manufacturing and Service Industries 1976*, HMSO 1978, pp. 8, 3.

10 The Way Forward

1. *I Only Work Here*, p. 142.

2. Working Together Campaign, *The Economic Facts of Life*, Databank International 1979.

3. See *The Universe*, 21 January 1980, p. 21.

old Niebuhr, *Moral Man and Immoral Society*, SCM Press
213f.
rkers' Participation in Management in Britain, p. 119.
imag, published in Mount Isa, June 1979, p. 8.
id., p. 7.